The
ITT Key Issues
Lecture Series

THE KEY ISSUES LECTURE SERIES
is made possible through a grant from
International Telephone and Telegraph Corporation

This series of lectures took place
at The University of Texas at Dallas
in Richardson, Texas

Private Enterprise and the New Global Economic Challenge

Edited by
Stephen Guisinger
Professor, Program Head
International Management Studies
The University of Texas at Dallas

With a Foreword by
Harold S. Geneen

Bobbs-Merrill Educational Publishing
Indianapolis

Copyright © 1979 by The Bobbs-Merrill Company, Inc.

Printed in the United States of America

All rights reserved. No part of this book shall be reproduced or transmitted in any form or by any means, electronic or mechanical, including photocopying, recording, or by any information or retrieval system, without written permission from the publisher:

The Bobbs-Merrill Company, Inc.
4300 West 62nd Street
Indianapolis, Indiana 46268

First Edition
First Printing 1979
Library of Congress Cataloging in Publication Data
Main entry under title:
Private enterprise and the new global economic challenge.

(The Key issues lecture series)
"Based on comments presented at the University of Texas at Dallas from October 1977 through March 1978."
1. International economic relations—Addresses, essays, lectures.
2. International business enterprises—Addresses, essays, lectures.
I. Guisinger, Stephen E.
HF1411.P677   382.1   79-11631
ISBN 0-672-97358-8
ISBN 0-672-97359-6 pbk.

Contents

Foreword

Harold S. Geneen

Chairman
International Telephone and Telegraph Corporation

Only a decade ago, the phrase "multinational corporation" was almost unknown. Having emerged since World War II, these large business organizations were just becoming an object for study within the academic community.

Today, multinational enterprises are the pacesetters for an unprecedented growth in world trade. They hold out the promise of spreading management skills and technological know-how to many millions of people who otherwise might not have these capabilities for generations to come.

Yet, some host governments of the less-developed countries (LDCs) seem to be caught in a "love-hate" syndrome. They want the constructive contributions to wealth and economic growth that the multinational corporations can provide to buttress their nations' power. At the same time, host nations may fear the results: the incursion of an independently controlled industry and the threat of technological dependence. However, there are constructive solutions to this dilemma, which often seems more emotional than economic.

I think these crosscurrents are symptomatic of change. More and more of the LDCs want to exert their growing influence in world markets. And I believe there is evidence the world is moving in the direction of even freer trade.

In his chapter, Dr. Moeen A. Qureshi of the International Finance Corporation stresses the importance of a "global compact" between the private and public sectors in the Third World. He notes that 75 percent of the gross domestic production of developing countries is supplied by the private sector.

Prof. Raymond Vernon, in another chapter, also touches upon this central theme. He calls for new alliances and new arrangements with national interests. He states that any host government which overlooks the potential of its private sector is depriving itself, and its people, of a strong vehicle for social advancement.

This book grew out of the second ITT Key Issues Lecture Series at the University of Texas at Dallas. It was written to assess the role that private enterprise should play in the international economic order. Our hope is that some of the ideas contained herein may suggest new approaches that can be translated into practical solutions.

For their splendid support of this effort, we are grateful to Dean Raymond P. Lutz, who organized the lecture series and Prof. Stephen Guisinger, who edited this book.

Introduction

Stephen Guisinger

Professor, Program Head
International Management Studies
The University of Texas at Dallas

For more than a century the private sector in the economy has steadily given way to the public sector. The share of goods and services produced in the United States today by government or directly under government control is greater than at any time in the past, except perhaps for World War II. The same trend is evident throughout the world, and the economic turbulence of the past decade has only accelerated this tendency towards greater public involvement in the economy, as governments have applied new restrictions in an attempt to contain inflation, reduce unemployment, and lend stability to exchange rates. Even the two most dominant features of the international economy in recent years—the multinational corporation and the Eurocurrency market, both products of the private sector—are under considerable critical attack, and calls for increased government controls are heard in several quarters.

The six essays in this volume address a common question of vital importance: What is the future role of private enterprise in the world economy? While it is clear that the private sector will always play *some* role, it is useful to examine carefully the nature and scope of that role and the conditions under which it is to be carried out. It is especially important to examine government controls over the private sector, which are of more concern to the private sector than direct government competition itself. The essays in this volume approach government involvement in the international economy from a variety of points of view. But one necessary point of departure for any examination of the future role the private sector is, of course, a clear understanding of the evolution of the multinational enterprise. Two essays in this series focus on that issue.

Raymond Vernon, professor of international business at Harvard University, depicts the current state of multinational enterprises as one of tension created by the opposition of two forces. One set of forces—the profit opportunities carved out by multinational firms on the basis of unique advantages in technology, size, or marketing information—propels firms abroad. Another set of forces—the desire of governments in host countries for a greater share of the benefits produced by these unique attributes—resists the expansion of multinationals. Vernon notes that, while the nationalistic sentiments opposing foreign investment have grown, so have the potential benefits to developing countries from the new technologies evolved by the multinationals. A precarious balance remains and is likely to persist into the future. What is certain, however, is that the multinational corporation will continue to be a convenient focal point for the frustrations of developing countries in their slow progress for modernity.

Richard D. Robinson, professor of international business at the Massachusetts Institute of Technology, examines the future of the multinational enterprise in what he terms the "resource-rich, technology-poor" countries, such as Saudi Arabia, Indonesia, and Nigeria. In Robinson's view, the days are clearly numbered for the "old-style" multinational firm based on integrated international production, equity control of subsidiaries, and a management dominated by the nationals of one country. The future belongs not to multinational *producers* but to international *suppliers* of inputs such as technology, skills, and market information. Thus, the likely evolution of the multinational is towards an unbundling of product and firm attributes. Robinson argues that a model for this exists today in the form of the Japanese trading companies. He concludes that this evolution is the natural result of the immense bargaining power that will be wielded by the resource-rich, technology-poor countries in the future.

Irving Kristol, professor of urban values at New York University, traces the decline of the private sector to a fundamental dissatisfaction with capitalism in liberal democratic societies. Societies today expect more from capitalism than it can deliver. Capitalism does not solve all of mankind's problems. It does not give meaning to life nor does it offer spiritual salvation. According to Kristol, these are more properly the responsibility of religion, but religion itself has been on the decline in Western society. Kristol argues that if we want an increase in material well-being, private enterprise should be left to do what it is most capable of doing—producing goods and services—and the provision of nonmaterial wants must be left to other institutions.

Mark Shepherd, Jr., chairman of the board of directors of Texas Instruments, surveys the recent economic performance of developed countries and finds that productivity growth, income growth, and technological expansion are closely interrelated. Where governments have restricted the flows of goods, capital, or technology abroad, productivity growth has suffered, which in turn has slowed income growth. What is needed to promote steady and noninflationary growth in the developed world is more liberal trade policies, a greater scope for private transfers of technology among countries, and increased incentives for private capital formation. As for developing countries, Shepherd finds their insistence on greater control over technology transfers to be misplaced. Inflows of foreign investment appear to precede rapid export expansion in developing countries, and the spill-over effects of foreign investment—i.e., the creation of labor skills, the local sourcing of supplies and raw materials—offer significant benefits that are frequently overlooked when governments decide to adopt restrictive foreign investment laws. In Shepherd's view, the private sectors in both developed and developing countries need to be strengthened, and he makes several recommendations to this end.

Moeen Qureshi, executive vice president of the International Finance Corporation, explores the question of the appropriate role for the private sector in developing countries. Ideologies, he notes, often obscure rational assessment of what the private sector can and should do to promote economic and social welfare. Too often, the contribution of the private sector is painted in black and white terms, whereas a more balanced assessment is warranted. Qureshi concludes that given the enormity of the development task ahead for the poorer countries and the predominant role already played by the private sector, few alternatives exist except to place considerable reliance on private sector expansion. To ease the tensions and defuse ideological polarities, Qureshi recommends, first, that the private sector recognize clearly the justified concerns of governments for the social and economic impacts of private sector growth, and, second, that governments avoid sudden shifts in the ground rules under which private sector entrepreneurs launch their investment efforts. In short, a new compact pledging the private and public sectors to cooperative development is needed. The experience of the World Bank Group suggests that such a compact is both feasible and desirable in the acceleration of economic growth in poor countries.

Paul Volcker, president of the New York Federal Reserve Bank, concludes from his survey of international capital markets that the private sector has been an indispensible part of the process of international financial intermediation. For example, without the existence of the Eurocurrency market, perhaps the purest form of private enterprise in operation in the world today, the sudden transfer of wealth resulting from the oil price increases would have been far more disruptive to the world economy than it actually was. One peculiar paradox identified by Volcker is that while private sector capital movements are regarded as mutually beneficial by both the creditor and debtor countries, restrictions on the mobility of capital—both direct and portfolio—exist and appear to be multiplying. To reverse this tendency, Volcker recommends that serious consideration be given to a General Agreement on International Investment patterned after the General Agreement on Tariffs and Trade. Volcker also argues that the risk of international investment should be reduced through expansion of International Monetary Fund resources, which would reduce the need of countries to resort to capital restrictions for balance of payments adjustment. New techniques of international lending, such as cofinancing, are also bringing the public and private sectors of the capital transfer together for more productive transfers of financial resources.

The six chapters in this volume are based on comments presented at the University of Texas at Dallas from October 1977 through March 1978 in the ITT Key Issues Lecture Series. I wish to thank the contributors for sharing their views on the role of private enterprise in the world economy. In so doing, they have helped to clarify issues that affect the economic future of developing and developed nations alike.

ONE

The Future of Multinational Enterprise in Developing Countries

Raymond Vernon

Professor of International Business
Harvard University

Anyone who is running fast can hardly be expected to spend much time puzzling over the long-run future. During the past few years businessmen with a large stake in developing countries have found themselves running very fast indeed. Long-term plans have often gone by the board, as those in charge responded to an ancient principle of planning: When the hare is being pursued by the hounds, its long-term plan is in deciding where next to jump.

The managers of multinational enterprises doing business in developing countries cannot be blamed if, from time to time during the past ten years, they have seen themselves as hares being pursued by hounds in full cry. At the beginning of that decade, in the latter 1960s, the managers of most multinational enterprises were able to contemplate their prospects in developing countries with some complacency. Brazil and Indonesia had just reversed their earlier policy of official hostility toward foreign-owned enterprises; Mexico had not yet experienced the unfriendly regime of President Luis Echeverría; India was being difficult as usual, but no more than usual; the oil sheikhs were troublesome, but not yet downright threatening. In Latin America, Asia, Africa, and the Middle East, foreign businessmen were expressing their sense of confidence by rapidly increasing their organizational commitments and their financial investments.

In the ten years that followed, however, many developing countries substantially revamped the visible rules of the game for the foreign-owned subsidiaries in their jurisdiction. On the face of it, such subsidiaries now seem to confront a much harsher environment in those countries. The multinational oil companies, for instance, have been dispossessed of formal title to most of their concessions and have assumed the role of managers, agents, or buyers for crude oil production in developing countries. The subsidiaries of enterprises in other lines, such as manufacturing, have been obliged to take on local partners to share their equity interests.[1] Some developing countries have placed severe limits on the rights of subsidiaries to remit dividends, interest, royalties, or other payments to their foreign parents. Moreover, foreign-owned subsidiaries have found themselves the targets of an increasing flow of demands from national authorities: demands that they place a lid on prices, limit their imports, increase their exports, use more local labor, or borrow less local capital.

A central question for managers of multinational enterprises who want to think in long-run terms is whether there are any predictable patterns to be encountered in the developing countries. Are they doomed to continue to play the role of hare in an endless game of hare and hounds, shifting their strategy with every new threat? Or are there some abiding elements in the game, elements that managers can count on in developing a longer-term strategy?

My view is that, despite the sudden ups and downs in the relations between multinational enterprises and developing countries, certain aspects of those relations have been fairly sustained and predictable. Moreover, these regularities seem just as likely to prevail in the future as they have in the past. Two sets of such regularities can be identified: one set relating to changes in the state of competition that multinational enterprises are likely to confront in the developing countries; the other set, not altogether independent of the first, relating to the way in which developing countries' attitudes toward multinational enterprises in their jurisdiction are altered in the course of time.

THE COMPETITIVE SETTING

As numerous studies have repeatedly affirmed, enterprises that establish producing facilities in foreign countries generally think of themselves as possessing some unique capability that distinguishes them from local firms and allows them to overcome the handicaps of foreign status.[2] In the ordinary course of events, the subsidiary of a foreign-owned firm located in a distant land confronts some special handicaps: the difficulties of doing business in another culture, perhaps even in another tongue; the difficulties of communication at long distance between a producing facility and headquarters; the discriminations, both subtle and obvious, that are practiced almost everywhere against a recognized "auslander"; and the special risks that always go with the crossing of international boundaries, including variable exchange rates and uncertain trade barriers.

So the enterprise that spreads its facilities beyond its national borders must perceive itself as also possessing some offsetting strength, some strength that will allow it to hold off competitors that are free of the foreigner's handicaps. Strengths such as these fall into a number of fairly well-defined categories. Some firms see themselves as leaders in the development and introduction of new products or in the management of intricate production processes, as in chemicals or advanced electronics. Some base their strength on sheer size—the size of their organization, the size of their financial resources, or the size of their distribution network; the aluminum and automobile firms, for instance, fall in this category. Some firms rely on an outstanding trade name, as in the case of food products and soft drinks. And some depend upon a well-developed international information-gathering capability, as in the case of international banking and international consulting.

As a rule, the developing countries that welcome foreign-owned subsidiaries into their jurisdiction are looking to draw some benefits from these strengths. Their needs, however, are usually expressed in somewhat different terms—typically, in the familiar trilogy of capital, access to markets, and human skills. In recent decades, as developing countries have turned to the hard tasks of industrialization and modernization, they have frequently found what looked like an easy fit between their own pressing needs and the capabilities of multinational enterprises. If the task was to explore some promising oil-bearing formations, multinational enterprises were generally at hand offering to provide the technology, the capital, and even the foreign markets. If the need was to produce tractors or radios for local consumption, multinational enterprises were prepared to mobilize the money, organization, and skills to perform the task.

This brings us to the first of the regularities on which multinational enterprises may be able to shape their long-run plans. Many of the strengths that give multinational enterprises their special position in developing countries are greatest at the time when the subsidiary of the enterprise first establishes itself in the country; thereafter, as a rule, those strengths are on the decline. If the strength of the enterprise rests on an ability to mobilize capital for the creation of a large smelter or a vast mine, then the bargaining power of the enterprise takes a big drop on the day the smelter or the mine is opened. If the strength of the enterprise lies in its skill at discovering new sources of oil or ore, then its power trickles away as the discoveries are made. If the technical skills of the enterprise are in production, as in the operation of a steel mill or a canning plant, then the strength begins to ebb as local technicians absorb the necessary skills.

Some strong suits of the multinational enterprises are, of course, less vulnerable than others. In some industries, such as industrial electronics, the pace of technological change is so rapid that developing countries are confronted with the need to absorb successive waves of technology and, accordingly, never quite seem to catch up. In other industries, although the technology may move at a more sedate pace, multinational enterprises sometimes have a firm hold on the international marketing channels for the product that their subsidiaries produce, as in the case of aluminum or automobiles. When that is the case, their ability to hang on may endure even after the technological edge is gone. Other multinational enterprises are in possession of trade names whose drawing power is so strong that developing countries are loathe to give up their right of access to such names, lest their own citizens complain or foreign customers turn their product down. In India, for instance, Coca Cola managed to endure thirty years of official hostility before it finally succumbed to a government that was prepared to face the displeasure of millions of Coca Cola drinkers.

Still, ever since multinational enterprises first came into existence about one hundred years ago, they have had to confront the wasting of their original positions and the threat of expulsion from the countries in which they operated.[3] The phenomenon of the obsolescing bargain, as some have called it, could already be seen in Germany before 1860, when leading Germans began to complain over the foreign ownership of Germany's mines. It could be seen in Russia and Mexico before World War I, when governments that had eagerly invited foreigners to help develop their countries were already pressing them to give up some of their rights. By World War II, foreigners engaged in plantation agriculture, oil production, mining, public utility operations, and banking had already seen the first of a series of hostile nationalizations in the developing countries. After World War II, at the very time when multinational enterprises were spreading most rapidly into the developing countries, acts of nationalization and quasi-nationalization became endemic, involving many more countries and many more industries. By the early 1970s, such measures had become commonplace. Before asking what all this means for the future of multinational enterprises in developing countries, however, it will help to bring these acts of nationalization into a quantitative perspective.

So far, the aggregate position of multinational enterprises as a class in developing countries has been increasing, not declining. From the 1950s to the early 1970s, the subsidiaries of such enterprises had greatly expanded their positions in the economies of those countries, not only in absolute terms but also by relative standards. To be sure, there are indications that the rate at which the leading multinational enterprises have been adding subsidiaries in developing countries reached a peak in the latter 1960s. There is also some evidence that in the years following, the number of subsidiaries sold or abandoned by multinational enterprises was slowly increasing.[4]

But neither of these tendencies has been enough to reverse the position of multinational enterprises as a group, or to prevent them from expanding their share in the economies of the developing countries. In manufacturing, foreign-owned subsidiaries in developing countries have often come to represent one third or more of national output, and even more of the national output of the modern industrial sector. In the extractive industries, the statistical picture is complicated somewhat by changes in the relation of international oil companies to the governments of oil-exporting countries, especially by the replacement of old-fashioned concession agreements with long-term management contracts and co-production agreements; but, even in this embattled area, the role of multinational enterprise remains dominant.

Yet there is no gainsaying the fact that the typical multinational enterprise feels ill at ease, even diminished, in its position in developing countries. Given the seemingly continued strength of such enterprises as a class, how does one explain the change in mood?

Much of the answer, as I see it, lies in the fact that the phenomenon of the obsolescing bargain has been accelerated a little, propelled by the rapid improvement in international communication and by the attendant shrinkages of international space. Although multinational enterprises continue to enter the developing countries buttressed by special strengths, they have characteristically been followed in a relatively short time by other multinational enterprises claiming similar capabilities. Accordingly, the number of enterprises offering any given product or service in a developing country has tended to increase over time. That tendency has not been universal, of course; there have been cases in which multinational enterprises have made their entry into a developing country by buying a local venture or pushing local ventures out of business. For some 2,500 manufacturing subsidiaries that were established in developing countries by 180 U.S.-based multinational enterprises, about 38 percent represented acquisitions of going business; and for 1,800 such subsidiaries established by other multinational enterprises, the comparable figure was about 27 percent.[5]

Nevertheless, the typical case, as I have pointed out in detail elsewhere, has been an increase in the number of firms competing in the modern industries of the developing countries, not a decline.[6] For instance, in Brazil the number of subsidiaries of large multinational enterprises engaged in producing agriculture chemicals rose from two to ten between 1960 and 1970, while the number of subsidiaries producing drugs increased from seven to fifteen. In India during the same period, despite markedly different official policies, the number of agricultural chemical firms in which foreign enterprises had an interest went up from one to seven, and drug firms from thirteen to twenty-two.

Apart from the increase in the number of subsidiaries of large multinational enterprises, other factors have added to the competitive threat for individual firms. As improvements in international communication and international transportation have continued to shrink the distances between countries, a number of smaller firms have taken the plunge into the multinational arena. Many of these new ventures, like the larger firms that they were emulating, have had their home base in the advanced industrialized countries. But by the latter 1960s, industrial firms based in some of the developing countries themselves also were beginning to show signs of multinational spread. Subsidiaries based in Brazil, Mexico, India, Hong Kong, Taiwan, Israel, and other industrializing countries, numbering overall in the many hundreds, were found producing in other countries of the developing world.[7]

A quite dramatic growth in the number and character of other international arrangements has also increased the number of potential competitors. In some cases, national firms in developing countries have been acquiring the necessary experience and resources to compete directly with the subsidiaries of multinationals. When those national firms have lacked some ingredient such as foreign technology or access to a foreign market, they have typically found ways of buying the missing ingredient. In some cases, they have entered into licensing or agency agreements with producing firms in other countries; in other instances, they have bought the needed information from foreign engineering and technical firms. By one route or another, some of these firms have managed to place themselves in a position of effective competition with the multinationals, especially in well-established and mature product lines.

As a result of these various trends, leading multinational enterprises have had to accommodate themselves to the erosion of their original positions of strength in the developing countries. Even if the governments of developing countries were not showing increased misgivings about the activities of multinational enterprises, therefore, many of these enterprises would still have a lessened sense of security and stability, induced by increases in competitive market pressures.

The fact is, however, that governments in developing countries also have been learning how to profit from increases in the number of firms bidding to perform in their economies. This is perhaps most clearly illustrated by the climactic events in the international oil market from 1970 to 1975. In that period, Libya and other oil-exporting countries were remarkably effective in exploiting the anxieties of the independent oil companies and playing them off against the majors. Signs of that same tendency are seen from time to time in other industries, promising to accelerate the process of the obsolescing bargain.

THE FRUSTRATIONS OF GROWTH

Increases in competition are not the only forces that have threatened the position of the subsidiaries of multinational enterprises in developing countries. Other factors of a fundamental character also have been involved.

Over the past few decades, most developing countries have gone through the travail of creating or rediscovering a national identity as independent nations capable of exercising some control over their own future. Of the hundred-odd developing countries, more than half came into existence after World War II. Those that could claim a national identity over a longer period, located mainly in Latin America, North Africa, and the Middle East, have undergone a change in national self-perception no less profound than that of the wholly new countries.

Ironically, however, at the very time when political developments have given such countries the opportunity to think of themselves as independent nations, technological developments seem to be crowding them back into a state of continued dependence. All countries in recent decades have had to confront seemingly inexorable trends in international communication and transportation that appear to be shrinking international space. Everywhere, nations are rubbing up against one another more frequently and more intimately. More and more, they have found themselves dependent on one another's raw materials or capital or technology or markets. This increased interdependence is evident whether the countries concerned are rich or poor, developing or developed, socialist or capitalist. But with their special need to retain a sense of independence, developing countries have had particular difficulty in reconciling themselves to an increasingly interdependent world.

The increase in the presence of foreign-owned subsidiaries has been only one manifestation of the growth in the linkages of developing countries. Curbing or expelling these subsidiaries, therefore, has not been the answer to the increased sense of crowding that the developing countries are feeling. When India nationalized the foreign-owned refineries in her jurisdiciton, for instance, one could not say that India succeeded in reducing her vulnerability to interruptions in the supply of crude oil. Indeed, the opposite case would be as easy to sustain; as long as foreigners owned refineries in the Indian economy, each side was vulnerable to pressure from the other—the companies to the threat of nationalization, the government to the threat of an interrupted oil supply.

The special reaction of the developing countries to the linkages created by the foreign-owned subsidiaries, therefore, has to be explained in other terms. One explanation is the sheer visibility of such enterprises. When the dependence of a developing country is based on trade or licenses or loans, there are no bricks and mortar visible in the country to epitomize the dependence. When the dependence rests on continued operation of a foreign-owned plant or mine inside the country, however, the galling sense of vulnerability can be linked with a visible target.

The tendency to pin the troubling problems of dependence upon a visible target is greatly strengthened by the fact that most multinational enterprises have their home base in a rich industrialized country. In many instances, the home-base country, as seen from the perspective of the developing country, is the principal colonizing power, responsible for a past state of colonialism or quasi-colonialism. That linkage, for instance, has contributed to intense reaction of some Mexican and Brazilian leaders to U.S.-owned subsidiaries in their countries, and the reaction of some Indian leaders to British-owned subsidiaries in the Asian subcontinent. The special hostility reserved for Japanese-owned firms in the southeast rim of Asia, including Indonesia, Thailand, and the Philippines, can also be understood in that light.

But there are other problems associated with the subsidiaries of multinational enterprises, quite apart from their provocative visibility. For some of the intellectual elite of developing countries, including scholars and writers, two other factors play a considerable role.

One of these factors is the sense of being forced to swallow an alien culture in its entirety—of being compelled to adopt not only its creative, efficient, and productive aspects but its profligate, tawdry, and shoddy aspects as well. As a general rule, the subsidiaries of multinational enterprises in developing countries have offered goods and services that their parent companies first learned to make in their home countries. The goods and services selected for sale in developing countries as a rule were those that offered the highest promise of profit. The result is that, along with the wonders of aspirin and streptomycin, multinational enterprises have also conveyed the glad tidings of roll-on anti-perspirants, men's cologne, eye shadow of many hues, puppy biscuits, and profusely sugared breakfast foods. Along with the pick-up truck and the earthmoving tractor, those channels have promoted the joys of the luxury limousine and the hot-rod motorcycle.[8]

In the rich industrial societies where such products originate, the social cost to society may well be worth the pleasure they generate for their buyers. In any event, whether or not the rich nations benefit from such products, they are in a much better position to bear the cost. In developing countries, however, some leaders feel that the trivial and wasteful products and services of the richer industrialized countries are too costly for their poverty-stricken states to bear. In another era, perhaps, the leaders of such countries might effectively have barred such products from the country. But that option has become much more difficult to exercise in a world that is inundated with radio and television, and criss-crossed by packaged foreign tours. As the leaders see it, therefore, their ability to carve out an independent course of economic and cultural development is imperilled by the shrinkage of international space.

Still another pervasive concern of leaders in the developing countries has to do with the production techniques that multinational enterprises carry into the economies of such countries. The concern is obvious: Since most multinational enterprises initially developed their production skills in the environment of the rich industrialized countries, their techniques lean toward the copious use of capital and the parsimonious use of labor. In developing countries, on the other hand, capital is relatively scarce and labor relatively cheap, a fact that suggests a very different emphasis. Accordingly, developing countries are fearful that the technologies being put in place by the subsidiaries of multinational enterprises are inappropriate and wasteful, draining scarce national capital and contributing to national unemployment.

Although the concern of the developing countries is straightforward enough, the relevant facts turn out to be much more complex.[9] Some of the evidence suggests that the developing countries have a real basis for concern; but some points in quite a different direction.

The developing countries are right, for instance, in assuming that the world's main production technologies are created in response to the conditions of the industrialized countries. The leading techniques for manufacturing automobiles, producing chemical fertilizer, canning and freezing food, and so on, all have been shaped in environments very different from those prevailing in the developing countries. Moreover, multinational enterprises tend to concentrate their production activities in industries that are on the whole relatively capital-intensive—for instance, in chemical production more than in apparel manufacture, and in TV production more than in furniture manufacture. Finally, multinational enterprises tend to build relatively large plants, as compared with national producers, and it is a well-established fact that in a given industry, the efficient large plant tends to be more capital-intensive than the efficient small plant. Cumulatively, the effect of these factors has been to associate multinational enterprises with capital-intensive processes, to the seeming detriment of developing countries.

Here and there, to be sure, multinational enterprises recognize that conditions in a given developing country call for a production process that operates efficiently at lower capacities or that uses less capital and more labor than plants operating in richer and bigger markets. Responding to that fact, multinational enterprises sometimes select machinery and processes for their manufacturing operations in a developing area that would be considered obsolete in richer markets; indeed, they often resurrect and ship second-hand machinery to developing countries in response to local needs. Moreover, even when the multinational enterprises mechanistically assign their latest production machinery and techniques to a facility in a developing country, they generally modify the machinery and the techniques as they gain experience with local conditions.

Although leaders in the developing countries worry a great deal about the appropriateness of the production processes applied by the multinational enterprises, the policies adopted by their governments often exacerbate the problem, rather than reduce it. Consider, for instance, the incentives that many developing countries offer in order to attract foreign investors. These commonly include provisions for the accelerated depreciation of plant and equipment as well as the right to import capital equipment without payment of duty; both measures tend to bias the selection of production techniques toward higher capital-intensiveness. On top of that, developing countries have been known to prohibit multinational enterprises from importing used machinery, insisting on their right to have "the latest and the best." Finally, state-owned enterprises in developing countries are typically allowed to indulge their propensity to choose large capital-intensive facilities over existing alternatives. Meanwhile, a little—but only a little—has been done in developing countries to stimulate engineers and businessmen toward creating distinctive production processes more appropriate to the circumstances of those countries.[10] From all appearances, if left to their own devices, developing countries would do no better in the selection of appropriate technologies than the multinational enterprises have done.

In sum, from the viewpoint of leaders in the developing countries, the multinational enterprise provides a convenient focus and ready symbol for a wide range of problems: for the threat of hegemony from the great powers, for disappointment and frustration in failing to achieve a greater degree of economic independence, and for the dislocation, waste, and inequities of the development process itself. For some of these problems, the linkage with the multinational enterprise is evident; for others, it is much more tenuous. In the heated discussions of the past decade, however, that distinction has not carried much weight. Sometimes serving as a symbol, sometimes accounting for substance, the multinational enterprise has figured at the center of the developing countries' efforts to deal with their manifold problems of modernization and change.

THE FUTURE

Because multinational enterprises are inexorably linked to fears of hegemony, worries over industrialization, and reservations about private enterprise, the first task of anyone who is weighing the future of such enterprises in the developing countries is to speculate about the future of these larger concerns. Speculation can never claim to be scientific or rigorous; each of us has a personal set of views, based on experience and on a perception of the historical process. In the end, therefore, projections of this sort represent a statement of faith much more than an academic exercise.

How are developing countries likely to look on the risks of continued hegemony, that is, the risk that the big industrial powers—especially the United States—will continue to dominate the economic life of the developing world?

No doubt that concern will continue strong in many developing countries. But the visible trends suggest this will be a declining concern for the future, not an increasing one. The decline is expected, in part, because practically all developing areas are having some success in multiplying and proliferating their links to the rich industrial countries, as reflected both in trade and investment. Where strong colonial or quasi-colonial ties once existed, their impact is being diluted by the increasing presence of rival foreign interests. Latin American countries are managing to develop more robust links with Japan and Europe, African countries with Japan and the United States, and so on.

Developing countries exhibit another tendency which may lead to a decline in their concern over hegemony. In addition to diversifying their links with the industrialized countries, most developing countries appear gradually to be building up greater self-confidence in their foreign relations. Increased access to United Nations organizations and the international press, along with increased practice in playing the ancient game of coalition in international affairs, appears to have contributed to that sense of confidence. Although multinational enterprises may be burdened by various factors in the developing countries in the years ahead, the burden of being identified with a powerful hegemonic state may prove lighter than in the past.

Of course, history rarely moves in altogether straight lines, and one can easily conjure up possibilities for swift changes. If the United States, for instance, had rejected the proposed treaty over the Panama Canal, the traditional picture of the United States in Latin America as *el pulpo,* the octopus, could easily have regained some of its vividness and power and could readily have added to the difficulties of U.S.-based multinational enterprises. Despite risks of that sort, however, my guess is that the linkage between multinational enterprises and economic hegemony in the minds of the developing countries is likely to weaken.

An even more critical question for the future is whether the developing countries, moving beyond rhetoric and exhortation, will make significant efforts to control the pollution, corruption, waste, and inequities that mar the industrialization process. And, if they do, will the burden of regulation fall more heavily on multinational enterprises than on any other type of firm? On the record to date, one is tempted to be cynical. As a rule, developing countries have been notoriously laggard in dealing with such problems. Part of the slow reaction, to be sure, can be explained in terms of a lack of national expertise and manpower. But explanations of this sort are not quite enough. Many developing countries, for instance, do not even require that automobiles and trucks imported from industrialized countries carry the antipollution devices that would be required for sale in the originating country. Nor do they require that labels bear the information and warnings demanded in the country of origin. The factors that inhibit action by the developing countries in such cases have not been well researched. But it is implausible to assume that the multinational enterprises themselves have been mainly responsible for the inaction of authorities in the developing countries. Such inaction probably stems from national factors as well.

But what of the more fundamental possibility that at some future time private ownership of the means of production may be placed in jeopardy in the developing countries? On that basic issue, indications are quite mixed.

One sign of the pressures against privately-owned enterprise in the developing countries is a sharp increase in the number of subsidiaries of multinational enterprises that have been nationalized or expropriated in the past ten years; that number is far higher than at any time in the past.[11] Moreover, on the whole, state-owned enterprises are rather more important in developing countries today than they were, say, a dozen years ago. A few governments, such as Algeria, have prohibited practically all private ownership in the modern industrial sector. Other governments, notably India and Nigeria, have adopted official policies reserving important areas of their respective economies to state ownership. Still others, without adopting a precise policy on state ownership, have found it convenient to create quasi-monopolistic state-owned entities in industries that required especially large-scale facilities; Brazil, Mexico, and Venezuela have followed policies of this sort.

Yet the push in favor of state-owned enterprise on the whole has not been constant. In Indonesia and Ghana, for instance, commitments to state socialism in one regime have been reversed by successor governments. In Mexico and India, periods of relative growth in the state-owned sector have been followed by intervals of encouragement to the private sector. In fact, over the past few decades, the private sector has managed to expand in most developing countries, gaining in resources, experience, and confidence.

The inability of state socialism to sweep the field in the developing countries is due in some measure to the faltering performance of the state-owned enterprises that already exist. Rates of utilization of plant and equipment have been fairly low, not much lower, perhaps, than the rates common to privately-owned plants in developing countries, but low enough to suggest that state ownership is no sure answer for poor technical performance.[12] Another disconcerting aspect in the performance of state-owned enterprises in developing countries has been a widespread tendency to spend more than they earn.[13] Although money losses do not constitute sure evidence that the enterprises have failed to contribute to the national welfare, the losses represent an official embarrassment and pose a budgetary problem for many countries. Finally, state-owned enterprises have been involved from time to time in egregiously antisocial behavior; some have been involved in extensive corruption, others have been callous and intransigent in the handling of pollution problems, and so on.[14]

As a result of factors such as these, governments faced with choosing between a state-owned enterprise and a foreign-owned firm in the execution of an especially large or difficult project have found themselves at times choosing the foreign firm. For similar reasons, governments that have gone through the process of expropriating a foreign-owned subsidiary have frequently arranged to have its former owners carry on some of the subsidiary's functions.[15] The cold-blooded corporate treasurer of the multinational enterprise, assessing the economic effects of the shift in the firm's status from ownership of a subsidiary to seller of services under a contract, has often been surprised by the result: The

prospective earning power of the new arrangements, when compared with that of the old and when suitably adjusted for relative
risk, has represented no economic deterioration at all.

Commonly, too, state-owned enterprises with no previous links
to a multinational enterprise have reached out to the multinationals for help on one difficult task or another. Fifteen years ago, when
state-owned Petroleos Mexicanos entered into a joint venture with
DuPont to produce tetraethyl lead in Mexico, the incident was
treated as a major event in business history. Today, that kind of
arrangement is commonplace.[16]

REPRISE

All told, therefore, the ideological threat to multinational enterprises in developing countries is ambiguous and uncertain. What is
not at all ambiguous, however, is the phenomenon of the obsolescing bargain. The familiar basic principle still seems valid: Those
enterprises that appear most indispensable to the developing countries see multinational enterprises as most valuable at the time of
their entry, and increasingly dispensable as the years go on. The
increased vulnerability may be due to the fact that the developing
country sees itself increasingly able to carry on the activities of the
multinational enterprise without help; or it may be due to an
increase in the number of multinational enterprises prepared to
perform the same function.

But the phenomenon of the obsolescing bargain is not universal.
Changes in products, in technologies, and in markets present new
challenges for the developing country and periodically serve to
restore a multinational enterprise to its pristine bargaining
strength. Moreover, new alliances and new arrangements with
national interests, including state-owned enterprises, sometimes
complement the foreigner's capabilities and buttress the foreigner's position. It is out of this congeries of trends and possibilities that each multinational enterprise must build its strategies
in the developing countries.

NOTES

1. See for instance R. D. Robinson, *National Control of Foreign Business Entry* (New York: Praeger Publishers, 1976).

2. The standard references on this point are S. H. Hymer, *The International Operations of National Firms: A Study of Direct Foreign Investment* (Cambridge, Mass.: MIT press, 1976); R. E. Caves, "International Corporations: The Industrial Economics of Foreign Investment," *Economica*, February 1971, pp. 1–27.

3. For more on this point, see Raymond Vernon, *Sovereignty at Bay: The Multinational Spread of U.S. Enterprises* (New York: Basic Books, 1971), especially chaps. 2 and 6.

4. J. P. Curhan and others, *Tracing the Multinational: A Sourcebook on U.S.-based Enterprises* (Cambridge, Mass.: Ballinger Publishing, 1977), Tables 2–2–4 and 3–4–6.

5. From data compiled by the Harvard Multinational Enterprise Project.

6. Raymond Vernon, *Storm Over the Multinationals: The Real Issues* (Cambridge, Mass.: Harvard University Press, 1977), p. 78.

7. See for instance C. F. Diaz-Alejandro, "Foreign Direct Investment by Latin Americans," in *Multinationals from Small Countries,* edited by Tamir Agmon and C. P. Kindleberger (Cambridge, Mass.: MIT Press, 1977), pp. 167–196; and L. T. Wells, Jr., "The Internationalization of Firms from Developing Countries," in the same source, pp. 133–166.

8. See for example K. P. Sauvant, "The Potential of Multinational Enterprises as Vehicles of Transmission of Business Culture," in *Controlling Multinational Enterprises: Problems, Strategies, Counter-Strategies,* edited by K. P. Sauvant and N. Lavipour (Boulder, Colo.: Westview Press, 1976).

9. See for instance G. K. Helleiner, "The Role of Multinational Corporations in the Less Developed Countries' Trade and Technology," *World Development* 3, no. 4 (April 1975): 161–189; United Nations, Department of Economic and Social Affairs, *The Acquisition of Technology from Multinational Corporations by Developing Countries* (ST/ESA/12), prepared by W. A. Chudson and L. T. Wells, Jr., 1974; David Morawetz, "Employment Implications of Industrialization in Developing Countries: A Survey," *Economic Journal* 84, no. 335 (September 1974): 491–542; S. A. Morley and G. W. Smith, "The Choice of Technology: Multinational Firms in Brazil," Rice University Program of Development

Studies, no. 58 (Houston, Fall 1974); UNCTAD, "Technological Dependence," in *The New International Economic Order*, edited by K. P. Sauvant and Hajo Hasenpflug (Boulder, Colo.: Westview Press, 1977), pp. 271–275.

10. For illustrations of some of the progress achieved so far in this field, see Nicolas Jequier, *Appropriate Technology: Problems and Promises* (Paris: Organization for Economic Cooperation and Development, 1976).

11. United Nations, Secretary General, *Permanent Sovereignty Over Natural Resources* (A/9716 and Corr. 1), 1974, pp. 1–7 and Table 1; M. L. Williams, "The Extent and Significance of the Nationalization of Foreign-Owned Assets in Developing Countries, 1956–1972," *Oxford Economic Papers*, n.s. 27, no. 2 (1975): 267 and Table 3. For a detailed study on the nationalization of U.S. investments in raw material ventures, see Stephen Krasner, "Raw Materials, Investments and American Foreign Policy," unpublished (Los Angeles: U.C.L.A., 1976), chap. 5, pp. 6–7 and Table 4-1.

12. A.R.B. Amerasinghe, *Public Corporations in Ceylon* (Colombo, Ceylon: Lake House Investments Ltd., 1971), Table 1; A. Besant C. Raj, *Public Enterprise Investment Decisions in India* (Bombay, India: Macmillan Co., 1977), pp. 112–117.

13. Andrew Gantt and Giuseppe Dutto, "Financial Performance of Government-Owned Corporations in Less Developed Countries," *International Monetary Fund Staff Papers* 15, no. 1 (March 1968): 102–135; K. D. Walters and R. J. Monsen, "The Nationalized Firm: The Politician's Free Lunch?", *Columbia Journal of World Business*, Spring 1977, pp. 90–102. For further evidence on a national level, see A. Besant C. Raj, *Public Enterprise Investment Decisions in India*, pp. 22–28 and Table 2-3; A. R. B. Amerasinghe, *Public Corporations in Ceylon*, Table 2; R. Thillainathan, "Public Enterprises in Malaysia," *UMBC Economic Review* 12, no. 2 (1976): pp. 37–44.

14. See for instance "Slowed Development and Huge Losses are Pertamina's Legacy to Indonesia," *Wall Street Journal*, 11 February 1977, p. 19.

15. Richard Sklar, *Corporate Power in an African State: The Political Impact of Multinational Mining Companies in Zambia* (Berkeley and Los Angeles: University of California Press, 1975), p. 41; David Smith and L. T. Wells, Jr., *Negotiating Third World Mineral Agreements* (Cambridge, Mass.: Ballinger Publishing Co., 1975,), pp. 45–47; James Cook, "Taking the 'AM' out of Aramco," *Forbes*, 15 December 1976, p. 41.

16. Data generated by the Harvard Multinational Enterprise Project on joint ventures between U.S.-based multinational enterprises and foreign state-owned enterprises in developing countries indicate that such partnerships grew rapidly in number after 1965; that they appeared mainly in intermediate industrial products, such as chemicals and machinery; and that they were geographically quite widespread, although a notable number of cases appeared in a few countries, including Iran and Algeria.

TWO

The Transfer of Technology to the Relatively Wealthy, Resource-Rich, Technology-Poor Countries

Richard D. Robinson

Professor of International Management
Alfred P. Sloan School of Management
Massachusetts Institute of Technology

The special position of the relatively wealthy, resource-rich, technology-poor countries—for example, Iran, Saudi Arabia, and Venezuela—is becoming a rather important issue in the area of international business, particularly with respect to the international transfer of technology.

Before proceeding to the substance of this chapter, it is useful to define very carefully the subject to which it is addressed. A great deal has been written about the transfer of technology, and very few definitions offered. By transfer of technology, I mean the transfer of the human capacity to replicate, adapt, and further develop the technologies needed to provide goods and services perceived as useful in the country to which the transfer takes place, plus the skills required to apply the technology to production. I do not mean the simple process of selling a piece of capital equipment and the skills needed to operate it. One would have to include in my definition also the transfer of an understanding of the theory and design of the process or machine, the capability of adapting and further developing it, and the ability to use the technology effectively in production. This, I think, is really what spokesmen from the less-developed countries generally mean by the transfer of technology. Certainly in the North-South dialogue this definition very clearly stands out.

Several developments should be pointed out which seem to affect the total environment in which the international traffic in technology takes place. One is that there is a considerable body of thought, and indeed some evidence, that technological innovation is slowing, particularly in the United States, but also possibly elsewhere in the industrial world. A number of reasons are advanced for this apparent slowdown. I merely list them here, for they constitute a very large subject by themselves.

First, there is increasing government intervention and regulation which introduces delay, and hence added cost, in the introduction of new technology. Second, there is a decline in government support for research and development in the United States. Third, and possibly more important, the time span of planning, corporate and otherwise, has been shortened as a result of inflation. That is, there is a need for rapid pay-out. Research and development investment does not assure such; rather, it tends to produce a very long, delayed pay-out, which in an inflationary situation is not very attractive. Fourth, inflation has also induced a shortage of capital for important industries and has caused money problems for research-oriented universities and other research institutions.

As a fifth reason for the apparent decline in technological innovation, we must note labor opposition to the introduction of new technology, particularly in the face of sustained unemployment at intolerably high levels. This opposition lengthens the pay-out time for new technology, and hence the cost of that technology. Sixth, and a factor not so widely discussed, is the slowed introduction of new technology due to the increasing stock of fixed capital. That is, greater and greater investment is required to apply new technology in a meaningful way as the stock of fixed assets grows ever greater. Seventh, some feel that the intensely competitive nature of society at an interpersonal level, characteristic particularly of the United States, is not conducive to high levels of creativity. Especially in the context of complex technology and large organizations, where large group effort is required over long periods of time, the U.S. environment may not be the most supportive of innovation. Eighth is the fact that at least in the United States, corporations seem to be using secrecy to protect their technology rather than patents. When a patent is issued, the technology it includes normally becomes available to anybody who reads the patent application. One suspects that the patent itself thus becomes an important source of technological innovation as others study what has been done and proceed to innovate on that basis. In anticipation of that process, and for other reasons, it appears that more and more U.S. corporations are going the route of secrecy, which means, of course, that this technology is not available to others.

The slowdown in U.S. technology and innovation is especially noticeable relative to some other countries. For instance, by 1976, Japan was issuing three times as many patents as was the United States. Admittedly, this figure is not a strictly comparable statistic, because Japan issues patents, whereas the United States does not. Also, the tendency for U.S. companies to maintain secrecy rather than apply for patents may in itself have something to do with the rate of technological innovation in Japan. In addition, there has been an overall decline in the number of engineers and scientists in U.S. industry despite increases in the population. Finally, there has been a general slowdown in economic growth in many industrial countries. The question arises whether this is related to a slowdown in R & D, that is, in research and development investment. There is some indication that it may be. For example, there have been some studies relating R & D investment and enterprise growth. In Figure 2.1, note that in terms of sales growth, productivity (output per

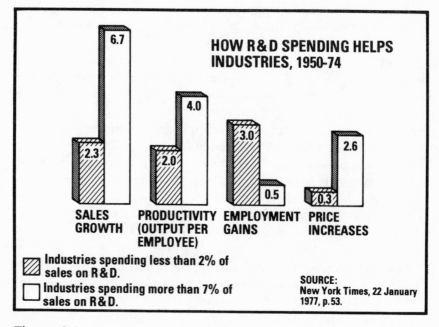

Figure 2.1

employee), and employment gains, the high investors in research and development outpace to a significant degree the low investors. The reverse occurs in the case of price increases; where the price increases were high, R & D investment was relatively low. These data suggest that there may be a causal link between research and development investment and the rate of economic growth. Although these figures relate to industry in the United States, there is no reason to expect a different pattern in industry located elsewhere.

The slowdown in U.S. technology and innovation relative to certain other industrialized countries is also evident in that the United States has been losing its share of world production in industry after industry. Table 2.1 shows the percentage of total

Table 2.1   Change in U.S. Share of World Production, 1960–74

Aerospace	+ 1.4%
Petroleum products	− 13.1
Food products	− 14.1
Paper and timber	− 15.6
Automotive	− 20.1
General machinery	− 20.6
Textile and apparel	− 21.7
Electrical equipment	− 25.1
Chemicals	− 36.0
Iron and steel	− 50.3
Mining and metals	− 56.3

Source: Calculated from tables in *New International Realities* (National Planning Association), July 1976, pp. 12–16.

world production in certain industrial sectors operating in the United States. Note that the percentage is based on change over the 1960 through 1974 period, a fifteen-year span, which indicates a significant shift in a remarkably short period of time. Along with this there has been a loss of U.S. market share as a percentage of total world trade. One also notes the more rapid growth of non–U.S.-based corporations. For instance, of the largest 486 corporations in the world in 1962, about 61 percent were headquartered in the United States. Ten years later that figure had dropped to 54 percent, again a significant change in a very short period of time. Hence, in speaking of the transfer of technology to the less-developed countries, we must think increasingly in terms of transfer from Japan, from the European Community countries, and from the Socialist Bloc, as well as from the United States.

Another development affecting international traffic in technology is that the poorer countries, the so-called group of 77, are rapidly developing a concerted position in respect to technology transfer. Indeed, in a 1977 meeting in Kuwait, held in anticipation of a U.N. conference in 1978 on technical cooperation among the less-developed countries, an international group of planners and experts, government representatives, and administrators produced a document which concluded, in part:[1]

> It must be recognized that traditional technical assistance has generally reinforced earlier forms of dependence. This has, in effect, tended to the stifling of self-reliant, national capabilities in developing countries. It has also led to incorporating developing countries into a scientific, technical, and economic system dominated by the highly industrialized world. Such experience has made it evident that self-reliant, national capabilities, responsive to national objectives and requirements, are fundamental prerequisites for viable development.

Reflected here is an insistence upon self-selection of the technology to be transferred. The document continues: "Self-reliance is not autarky. It is the will and capacity for autonomous decision making and execution in all areas of society and economy. Science and technology are essential elements of a self-reliant capability." In other words, there is insistence upon the development of one's own national capability for ordering the technological needs of a country and not simply following the lead of an external agency or foreign corporation. The conferees then pointed out that two dimensions are vital to the process of supporting national self-reliance. The first was the

> re-orienting of traditional technical assistance programs and practices, both multilateral and bilateral, through basic changes in approach and concept. Provision of skills and

technologies, readily available with public and private commercial companies of the industrialized countries to developing countries, in a traditional way, must be replaced by identification and evaluation, by the developing countries, jointly with their multilateral, bilateral partners, of all available techniques and technologies. The developing country concerned will then select the one regarded most appropriate by it.

Reflected here is a desire to improve the international market for technology by improving knowledge of the options and the capacity to select the technology deemed most appropriate. The second point relevant to national self-reliance was: "The expert equipment training package, as the basic instrumentality of technical assistance, must be replaced by selective acquisition of individual elements of that package." In other words, the technology package should be "unbundled." One might go on to mention the unbundling of the entire direct foreign investment package, that is the separation of investment from expertise, equipment, training, management, marketing, and capital—each input to be separately described and discretely priced. One notes that there are strong pressures around the world in this direction, particularly in the resource-rich countries. Associated with the unbundling notion is the forced spin-off of ownership-based control, the forced transfer of functions (such as domestic marketing), and the transfer of skills and technology (via training requirements and a variety of other devices).

The international climate in which the transfer of technology takes place is affected, then, by three developments: (1) the possible worldwide slowdown in technological innovation, which leads to rising competition among sources of technology; (2) the decreasing preeminence of the United States in world production and trade; and (3) the concerted effort by the poorer countries to improve the terms upon which they acquire technology.

Several problems arise in addressing the subject of technological transfer to the resource-rich, technology-poor countries. In the first place, these countries are not alike with respect to interests and policies. One is justifiably suspicious of generalizations as to what ought to be done, because even within the rather limited category of less developed countries—that is, the resource-rich, technology-poor—interests and policies vary substantially. Hence, they require different business responses. Further, the relevant policies of the industrialized countries—the technology suppliers—are not alike with respect to objectives and strategies, a fact which the countries purchasing technology should take into consideration. Another problem is trying to find a generalizable objective in this area. One can say that the overall objective is to reduce the cost and facilitate the transfer of appropriate technology with a minimum of continuing external—that is, foreign—control, but without discouraging technical innovation and its transfer. That is, private firms having the technology, or in a position to develop it, must see the transfer as sufficiently profitable so as to encourage them to innovate and make that technology available to others.

Underlying these general problems are certain fundamental questions that must be addressed: Can the cost of technology be reduced without destroying the stream of innovation, which may already be slowing, and the willingness to transfer that technology? Can institutions be devised which will facilitate the transfer of technology, and what should their functions be? What is "appropriate" technology? For what and for whom is it appropriate? And finally, how can control be minimized, when it appears that reduced control over the use of technology and its development simply increases its cost?

One needs to address these questions particularly in the context of the resource-rich, technology-poor countries. Insofar as reducing the cost of technology is concerned, the way not to do it—and I think many governments recognize this truth or are beginning to do so—is to try to force a loss of control over the technology by the supplying firm. That threat leads to high cost, not low cost. But one can generate lower cost by improving the international market for technology. How? One way is by providing better information as to the possible alternative technologies and their sources, all of which suggests access to information systems and data banks that contain this information, plus trained local people able to evaluate the alternative technologies in the local context. Another way costs might be reduced is by more adequate financing of private international trade in technology and associated skills and services. We have invented a whole host of institutions financing trade in commodities, but it is very difficult for firms to find adequate financing for trade in technology, skills, and services. Very few institutions are willing to supply substantial finance, or to share the risks involved, at a reasonable cost. What about designing institutions to facilitate transfer? We are really talking again about reducing costs when we speak of institutions which provide better information, better evaluation of existing technologies around the world, and more adequate financing.

As to the "appropriateness" of technology, the term is meaningful only if one talks about increasing technological options. If there is only one option, the term is meaningless, and potential buyers are faced with a take-it-or-leave-it situation. So, one refers to increasing options and making these options known—options such as reducing the economies of scale; using different materials, more labor, less energy, or different technological specifications; or, dividing processes into technological modules which have different characteristics in these several respects, and then recombining the modules. One suspects that as markets become increasingly international, which, of course, is happening as the world economy becomes better integrated and national economies become more interdependent, more corporate sensitivity will surface with respect to the need for research and development addressed to the particular technological requirements of foreign markets. Hence, technological options are very likely to increase.

The key question about appropriate technology is, of course: Appropriate for what and for whom? Technology may be appropriate by virtue of being rational in some limited economic sense. But at the same time, it may not serve other equal or more important needs, such as maintaining employment, producing a standardized quality product, generating national pride and national cohesiveness, protecting the environment, conserving expendable resources, generating a sense of participation in the scheme of things, effecting a more equal distribution of income, protecting the consumer, or protecting labor. All of these are perfectly acceptable objectives, and the technology chosen may have an impact upon them. So, the definition of what is appropriate is a very flexible one depending upon the specific priorities and needs of a particular society. What we are really talking about, then, is the knowledge and skill required *to produce something a society wants in a way acceptable to that society.* Without revealing its system of priorities to the outside world, a society must develop the skill to translate those wants or needs into technological specifications. Indeed, this suggests a possible international institution to assist in that evaluation process.

Another question posed above had to do with minimizing continuing external control by a foreign enterprise or government over the use and further development of a transferred technology. For instance, the originator of a technology may seek to control its use in manufacturing exports, or limit the level of production, or refuse to permit local adaptation. Naturally, the host society generally finds it desirable to minimize this external control.

Reserving further comment on this issue until later, let us readdress the problems one must face in discussing the transfer of technology: the differences among resource-rich, technology-poor countries which lead to differing policies; the widely ranging interests and policies of the technology-producing countries and their various enterprises; and, finally, the problem of specifying a generalizable objective at an operational level.

Looking just at the differences among the resource-rich, technology-poor countries, one is led to inquire why they differ and how they differ. In the first place, the ability of these nations to extract a relatively high rent from the rest of the world for their resources differs enormously from one to another. This rent is relatively high in terms of the goods and services a nation has to buy. With the exception of the oil producers, the resource-rich nations have not been able to push prices up *yet.* In the long run,

however, a massive shift of financial resources is likely to occur to
the benefit of a whole new group of now poor, but resource-rich
countries. These countries also differ in terms of relative wealth,
that is, the level of wealth in comparison to need. Even some of the
oil-rich countries—Iran, Nigeria, Indonesia—although they seem
fantastically wealthy and are members of OPEC, are nonetheless
borrowing heavily from the rest of the world. Their populations
remain large and poor, quite unlike those of Saudi Arabia, Kuwait,
or the United Arab Emirates, where per capita incomes are incred-
ibly high. There are also differences in technological sophistication, that is, in the absorptive capacity of these countries, or the
speed and ease with which their people can acquire new skills and
new technology. For example, a Venezuela is very different from a
Nigeria on this score. Also, the size of the internal markets of these
countries varies; a Saudi Arabia differs, obviously, from an Iran or
a Venezuela. One might point out that a wealthy resource-rich
country with a potentially large internal market has far greater
leverage vis-à-vis a foreign business than does a country with a very
small internal market. As a result of these varying national characteristics, one can expect priorities to differ, and, hence, policies
and attitudes with respect to foreign capital, employment, basic
education and technical training, export markets, and continua-
tion of foreign ownership and equity-based control.

A second problem, one may recall, had to do with differences
among enterprises in the industrialized countries. This subject is
not adequately addressed in the popular literature on technology
transfer, nor, indeed, in much of the professional literature. The
problem really has to do with differing degrees of responsiveness
on the part of business to national priorities, as signalled by flexibility of strategies. Why should responsiveness vary from one enterprise to the next? Let us consider some of the differences. Take a
corporation based in a small country versus a corporation based in
a large country. Is there a difference in their behavior and how they
are perceived in the Third World? A firm based in a large continen-
tal market, such as the United States, may well exhibit less sensitivity to the differing political, economic, and social priorities of

another country. Hence, it will be less flexible in terms of its strategic responses, that is, its willingness to "unbundle" the enterprise package (consisting of equity capital, debt, technology, skills, marketing, organization, management—all of the inputs) and its willingness to sell these, not on the basis of *ownership,* but on the basis of *contract.* In contrast, a firm based in a small national market is likely to be more sensitive and more flexible. Furthermore, it is likely to enjoy much greater support of its parent government, because export trade is perceived to be vitally important. If forty to sixty percent of a nation's Gross National Product is derived through international trade, the government naturally supports activity that encourages the enlargement of these flows, and it is willing to share the risk to a certain extent. This difference in parent government support may place the large-country corporation in a non-competitive situation in terms of some of the new business relationships that are emerging.

Differing perhaps even more importantly is the industrialized country in which the marketing and manufacturing functions tend to be separated. In such a country international marketing is done largely by entities other than the manufacturing enterprises; the marketing or trading company does the international buying and selling, not the manufacturer. That country's primary interest may well be in stimulating the flow of goods and services, not in owning factories—producing units—around the world. They prefer to have others manufacture, but are willing to get things started. This they might do by providing certain entrepreneurial high-risk capital to initiate an activity, but withdrawing it as rapidly as possible, and then supplying the necessary technology, skills, debt capital, and, more importantly, access to international information and distribution systems. Their earnings derive from those flows, not from dividends as in the case of direct investment. We have described in essence the general trading company model, most characteristic of Japan, an enterprise quite unlike the multinational corporation in its organization, international linkages, and behavior. It is, one suspects, significant that recent growth patterns of the ten big Japanese trading companies, in terms of the value of goods and services handled, show twice the rate of growth of the larger multinational corporations. Furthermore, these trading companies are increasingly moving into international traffic in technology and associated skills.

So, we have differences among the resource-rich, technology-poor countries, among the supplying countries, and among the technology-supplying enterprises. Differences among countries lead to differing national priorities and policies. Differences among enterprises lead to differing corporate responses and strategies—for example, in terms of willingness to withdraw from equity-based control, willingness to sell technology and skills via contract, willingness to allow independent national manufacturers entrée to an international distribution system, willingness to transfer technology effectively by transferring the associated skills to use and adapt the technology in the local context, and willingness to develop technology which is a close fit to the needs and desires of a particular country (the mini-plant, the more labor-intensive technology, and the like). All these differences make it difficult to provide valid generalizations at a detailed level.

One can, however, see a distinct tendency, particularly for the resource-rich, technology-poor countries, to "shop around"—to find the enterprises willing to enter into "turn-key plus" or similar types of contracts, those not insisting on ownership and continuing control, but willing to transfer the technology in terms of developing appropriate local skills. What this suggests is the compelling need for flexible corporate policies to conform to host countries' perceived needs. It also suggests, I suspect, lower risk and higher profit for the corporations entering into such contracts. Admittedly, some loss of control over fixed assets may follow from these strategies, but there is a serious question here: Is a company a profit maximizer or is it merely satisfying some profit threshold and maximizing control without justifying that control in terms of lower risk and higher profit? Bear in mind that another word for control is power.

It is not up to the supplying firm to judge whether a host country's perceptions as to its needs are good, bad, or indifferent, except, of course, if that government's policy is obviously at odds with a society's own priorities. In that event the firm had better hedge in anticipation of a shift in policy. This sensitivity to national priorities requires highly sophisticated analytical skills on the part of corporate management.

My own prognosis is to expect the disappearance of the large multinational corporation from the less-developed countries generally, if by multinational corporation we mean equity-based control over an internationally integrated production system, managed and owned centrally by the nationals of the country in which the parent company is domiciled. It is important to bear this definition in mind, because many writers, and people in the United Nations, talk very loosely of the multinational corporation (the *transnational,* in U.N. parlance). The multinational corporation, as it has appeared after World War II, is a distinctive type of international business organization characterized by these elements: (1) equity-based control; (2) an internationally integrated production system; (3) parent-company management and ownership preeminently by the nationals of one country; and (4) domicile of the parent corporation in that country with which its managers and owners are identified. Historically, that is what is meant by multinational corporation; a difference in any one of these dimensions implies a different type of business organization and one behaving quite differently.

I suggest that the future of international business may well belong essentially to the purveyors of technology, skills, and access to global information and marketing systems. In part, this will be because of the pressure which is now being generated by the resource-rich, technology-poor countries. I suspect that the general trading company model, although that phrase is an unfortunate choice, most nearly fits the need of many of these countries in terms of flexibility of response. And it is the resource-rich, technology-poor countries which are generating much of the pressure against the multinational corporation, because these countries can afford to assume the financial risk themselves. They have the wherewithal to assume that risk, so that the risk-bearing capability of the multinational corporation is no longer important to them. They can avoid, then, equity-based control. If their internal market potential is significant, that pressure becomes much greater, because the attraction of the corporation to the lucrative internal markets of these countries becomes compelling.

Consider what general trading companies do. They sell entrepreneurial high-risk capital, withdrawn as rapidly as possible in favor of local ownership. They sell high level skills and technology. They sell information. They sell access to global marketing systems. And it is the general trading companies of Japan, at least the largest of them, who *now* have the relevant data banks which give one access to the world's technology available to private parties for a price. The relevant information systems are in place. One suspects therein lies our principal competition. To some extent, companies of other nations are trying to emulate the Japanese in this regard, and, indeed, if the major trading companies were not Japanese, they might be able to operate somewhat more freely. But at this moment, the Japanese enjoy an enormous headstart in terms of technological data banks, information systems, and flexibility of response.

The shift of wealth to the resource-rich countries, as resource prices increasingly reflect their finite limits, forces the issue. These countries, one might add, have compelling internal political pressures, very commonly including a high degree of suspicion of the political motives of the industrialized countries, whether socialist or capitalist. They will not tolerate continuing foreign control, and they have the means to avoid it. Consequently, the multinational corporation, as I define it here, is a dying institution at least in the less-developed countries, the leading edge of which are the resource-rich, technology-poor countries.

One might ask *should* the multinationals disappear? Should the trading company model become the preeminent form of international business, including technology transfer? All one can say is that when we speak of the appropriate role of private international business, we are really speaking about the degree to which the activity of such enterprises is perceived to support national priorities of both the host and parent countries—or could be made to support national priorities, given the right policies on the part of the relevant governments. On the one hand, we have the host country's government intervening to influence the flow of human, physical, and financial resources in order to achieve national objectives, whatever they may be. On the other hand, there is the response of foreign firms to such intervention. Such firms control the necessary external inputs, in this case technology and associated skills and capabilities. Will they seek to maximize profits, or simply to maintain control, that is, power? How to bring the interests of these two groups into harmony constitutes the essence of the problem, and the issue is brought into focus in the resource-rich, technology-poor countries.

NOTE

1. As reported in *Action UNDP,* September/October 1977, p. 5.

THREE

Capitalism versus Anticapitalism:

The Moral and Political Issues

Irving Kristol

Professor of Urban Values
New York University

The question I wish to explore is this: Why is it that the economic/social/political system which I call liberal-democratic capitalism does not get the two cheers which it does, in fact, merit? On the contrary, it gets a great deal of harsh and, I believe, unfair criticism. I should like to elucidate the virtues of the system, for no system has even been as badly defended as the one we call liberal capitalism. I would also like to suggest why a great many people very knowingly detest it, not because they do not understand it, but because they do understand it and dislike what their understanding tells them.

I have used the phrase "liberal-democratic capitalism" and those three terms, in my view, are connected. But it is important to be precise about the nature of that connection, because otherwise one gets into a great deal of confusion. It is possible to have a capitalist economic system—that is, an economy predominantly guided and determined by the market—without having a liberal or democratic political regime. There are many such instances in the contemporary world. We do have regimes that have primarily a market economy but that are authoritarian, to one degree or another. So the existence of a market economy is no guarantee of a liberal-democratic society.

On the other hand, capitalism or a predominantly market economy does seem to be a necessary if not sufficient condition for a liberal-democratic polity. There is no regime in this world, and there never has been a regime, which was liberal-democratic and did not have a predominantly market-oriented economy. One can have the market economy without liberalism or democracy, but one cannot have a liberal democracy without the market economy. This was perfectly understood by the founding father, as it were, of modern capitalism, Adam Smith. Smith urged the capitalist system upon his fellow men not only because it would create greater wealth and engender greater economic efficiency, but also because it established a precondition for a liberal society. True, he was not thinking specifically of democracy in 1776—no one really was—but of a regime that would be, by any relevant historical standards, respectful of individual liberties. By its very nature, a limited government of this kind had to be more responsive to public opinion than any more authoritarian regime.

So there is a connection between that economic system we call capitalism—which one may define quite simply, after Robert Nozick, as an economic system consisting largely of commercial transactions between consenting adults—and those political regimes which respect the rights of men and the rights of the individual. A failure to see this connection leads to all sorts of foolish statements and foolish behavior on the part of our policy makers. President Carter's campaign on human rights is such an instance.

Now, obviously, any American presidency, any American administration, must stand and should stand for human rights. But when you stand for human rights you cannot assume, as I fear this administration does, that human rights are gifts of government—and then procede to criticize foreign governments, demanding, "Why don't you give your people human rights?" Human rights are not gifts of government. If they are gifts of government, government can take them away. To secure human rights you need *limited* government, not *benevolent* government. The founding fathers of this nation, in order to secure human rights, took great pains to set up a system of limited government—a system consistent with, and made possible by, the capitalist economic system which the founding fathers also envisioned.

In other words, if you really are serious about human rights, if you want other nations to respect human rights, you do have to take two things seriously. First, you have to take their economic system seriously. There is no point in telling the Soviet Union to observe human rights while remaining communist. It cannot. There never has been, in all of human history, a political regime based on that kind of economy which respected human rights. To establish an enduring respect for human rights you need a predominantly market economy, because it is the market economy that diffuses power, diffuses wealth, diffuses authority, creates that "social space" within which individual freedom flourishes. And in addition to capitalism—which is only, as I say, a necessary but not a sufficient condition—you need limited government, that is, government structured so as to place inherent limits on its power over the individual citizen. That is what you need to get human rights. That is what the founding fathers understood. That is what everyone understood until recent decades when, somehow, the notion of human rights came to be seen as something that is conferred by a benign and paternalistic government.

We are in the position today, I regret to say, of going around the world asking dictators to give their citizens human rights. Now, they may do it, for one reason or another. But they also may do it only temporarily. For human rights to take root and flourish you need a predominantly capitalistic economy, and you need a political system that accepts limited government as legitimate. One of the reasons so many of our writers and so many people in Washington (in both parties, incidentally) do not see this is because it would be very inconvenient for them to see it. The fact is that a great many people who now say they are for human rights here, there, and everywhere, are *not* in favor of limited government. They are not in favor of limited government because they want government to move more decisively in the direction of managing the economy. They want to see political power further centralized, rather than diffused, in order to achieve their goals of equality or equity or justice or whatever. To the degree that we have lost our commitment to the market economy, to the degree that we have lost our commitment to the idea of limited government, our campaign for human rights is going to be nothing but empty rhetoric.

I make this point, not out of a desire to be quarrelsome about Mr. Carter's foreign policy, or anyone's foreign policy, but to emphasize that there is a connection, an important connection, between that economic system which we call capitalism and that political system we call liberal democracy. Unfortunately, the perception of this connection has been much weakened in recent decades, so that we have now a great many people—especially young people—who dream that it is really possible to have a liberal democratic regime with a noncapitalist economic system. The interesting question is why they are able to believe this, because, as I have noted, it has never existed. History tells us with summary authority that you do not get freedom in the political sphere unless you also have a great deal of freedom in the economic sphere.

Nevertheless, a great many intelligent and sincere people are now convinced that such a society—a liberal polity with a state-controlled economy—can indeed exist. Why do they believe this? Why are they moved to demand what history says is, at the very least, highly improbable and perhaps impossible?

Some would say it is because the economic performance of capitalism is so very disappointing. Well, the answer to that accusation against capitalism is the same as in the old joke: "How's your

wife? Compared with what?" In what sense is the economic performance of capitalism disappointing? Compared with what? With
the performance of the Soviet economy? With the performance of
some other existing species of economy? The fact is that, on the
whole, we do better than others, not worse. Look at the economic
history of the Soviet Union. Ever since the Russian Revolution six
decades ago it has become ever more clear that that kind of economic system is indeed capable of doing certain things, above all in
the military area. The ancient pharaohs of Egypt could build
pyramids, the rulers of the Soviet Union can build steel plants,
airplane factories, and tank factories—but they cannot create an
innovative, dynamic economy that consistently, over the longer
term, improves the average person's standard of living. To have
such an innovative, dynamic economy you need what Schumpeter
called "creative destruction." Innovation is very upsetting. It de-
stroys existing products. It perplexes existing institutions. It unset-
tles existing habits. Where the government controls the economic
system, it resists such innovation, which it perceives as a threat to
political stability.

The Soviets are a very gifted people. They produce superb
scientists. Yet if we were asked to name some interesting new
products that have come out of the Soviet Union in six decades, I do
not think we could come up with one. There is little innovation in a
society run by a centralized bureaucracy. The bureaucracy is resist-
ant to innovation. It is painful to them; they have too much to lose.
The result is that, as concerns the standard of living of the Russian
people, the Soviet economy has performed poorly over these past
six decades. Other economies of a socialist inclination have also not
performed notably well. In the so-called "less-developed" countries
we have a full range of regimes, some capitalist, some semi-
capitalist, some noncapitalist. How do they fare? The answer is
clear: The more capitalist they are, the better off they are economically. Look at the economic performance of South Korea as
compared to that of North Korea. Look at Taiwan and Communist
China—again, no question as to which has the superior economic
performance, the superior economic growth. Or, in Africa, look at

the Ivory Coast. It is doing very very well economically. Next door to it, the socialist nation of Ghana is doing very very badly. In every case, as you look at the spectrum of these "less-developed" countries, those with predominantly market economies are in reasonably good shape. They grow much more rapidly, they produce more wealth, they make everyone better off, they permit everyone—as Adam Smith put it—to "better his condition."

This is one of the incontestable facts of the past three decades. If you want to surmise how a country is faring economically, look at its economic system. The more capitalist it is, the better it does.

Some of my colleagues in the academic world will have all sorts of fanciful explanations for this fact—extremely subtle, extremely learned, and all beside the point. Economics is a very simple, indeed vulgar, subject and the truth about economics is also very simple. To the degree that people wish to better their conditions, economics always tells the same old story: Give people the incentives, take the political obstacles out of the way, and they will better their conditions. It does not matter whether these people are Japanese, Chinese, Hindu, or Eskimo. The formula always works. One can read sophisticated analyses of Hindu culture, indicating that it frustrates economic development in India. All I know is that the Indians who leave India take their culture with them. They go to Britain or to Africa, and they make great economic progress. In many of the so-called backward countries, where you hear it said "There must be something in their cultural traditions that is frustrating their economic growth," it turns out that it is always government that is frustrating their economic growth. The reason India does not grow any faster is because the government keeps fouling up the economic system.

I do not wish to imply that culture is unimportant. Differences in culture make for differences in the *rate* of economic growth. Because of such differences, Germans and Swedes seem always to do better than, say, Spaniards or Portuguese. Nevertheless, when the Spanish or Portuguese governments get out of the way, Spaniards and Portuguese do quite well too. In recent years, we have had a rather large Portuguese migration to New Jersey. These poor people seemed unable to manage their economic affairs back in Portugal; yet they come to New Jersey—which, Lord knows, is not a land of milk and honey—and they all do fine in short order. In Spain or Portugal they seem to lack the "Protestant ethic," that is, the commercial ethic. In New Jersey, they soon go into business and prosper—because government permits them to.

So, looking at the record of economic performance, if one is interested in people improving their material conditions, living longer, eating better, having more choice as to how to spend their money and lead their life, capitalism is the obviously preferred system.

However, it might be asked, what about the inequality of wealth and income that economic growth under capitalism generates? On this matter, there are some absurd misconceptions abroad—misconceptions about the degree of inequality in this country today as compared with any other country at any other time. To begin with, practically all the statistics one sees on inequality of income in this country are nearly meaningless. Rarely are they corrected for important factors such as the "in-kind" income of the poor (e.g., food stamps, free medical care, subsidized housing) and especially age. It makes no sense to say one-fifth of the population earns this much, one-fifth of the population owns that much, or the top fifth gets such-and-such a percent of the national income, without knowing the age of the people in the different fifths. When I read some of the learned papers on the distribution of income, I discover that my son, who is a teaching assistant at Harvard, is close to the lower fifth. Well, that makes no sense. He is not near the lower fifth at all. It just happens that he is a young man who, for a period of time, has to be careful about making ends meet. The fact that his apartment is shabby or that he cannot afford a car is of no significance, since one of these days he surely will be living much better.

Until and unless they can be corrected for age—and we have not figured out a way to do that, statistically—most of the statistics about the various fifths of the American population are close to meaningless. They may tell nothing more than that a man of fifty is going to have a much higher income than a man of twenty. Yes, of course he will. Is that a problem? Is it "unfair" that a man of fifty, at the prime of his career, should be earning more money than a young man just beginning his career?

I am fond of telling my students that if you need a sociologist to tell you whether or not you have social classes in a country, you do not have social classes in any meaningful sense of the term. Where social classes really exist, common opinion is quick to recognize them. Similarly, if you need an economist to tell you that you have a problem of inequality in a country, you do not have a real problem of inequality. Most Americans, in truth, do not think inequality is a terrible problem in this country. Some politicians do, some academics do, but the average American does not. He knows, of course, that some people are richer than he is. He knows that Nelson Rockefeller and Roger Staubach and Robert Redford make much more money than he does. It does not especially bother him, for he also knows that he has improved his economic condition during his lifetime, and that his children will probably do likewise. In a democracy that experiences sustained economic growth, there is likely to be less envy, not more. It is stagnation that breeds this self-destructive emotion.

In any case, inequality is always relative. The real question is by what historical benchmark we are going to measure inequality in capitalist America. There has been some interesting research on historic inequality. I would especially recommend the neglected book by Jean Fourastié, *The Causes of Wealth*. Fourastié traces the distribution of income in France from the Middle Ages through the Renaissance to the present—and modern bourgeois society turns out to be far more egalitarian than any of its predecessors. Actually, we knew this all along. Has anyone ever really believed that the American worker today is poorer, vis-à-vis his employer, than the peasant of the seventeenth or eighteenth century vis-à-vis his landlord? To be sure, it is easy to *imagine* a society more equal than ours—and nicer in every way, for that matter. But mature men and women do not go around comparing actual societies with ideal societies, any more than they go around always comparing actual spouses with imaginary, ideal ones—that way lies madness.

It might be said that, while unequal *earnings* do not of themselves violate any principle of social justice, differences in *inherited* wealth do indeed constitute a kind of inequality that is problematic. Is it really "fair" that some people should inherit a large sum of money and other people should inherit nothing? That is an interesting theoretical question, not to be lightly dismissed. The trouble with trying to cope with this question on a practical level, however, is that inherited wealth is closely connected with the institution of the family. It is very difficult to persuade parents not to give their children "every advantage" and not to leave their children as much money as they can. Andrew Carnegie, incidentally, took a dim view of inherited fortunes. He felt they were a violation of the ethics of the capitalist system. He thought rich people should give all their money to charity and philanthropies, leaving their children to start at the bottom and work their way up—not a bad idea, perhaps, though it is easier for those who have neither money nor children to contemplate. For better or worse, parents do tend to love their children more than they love other people's children, and they do want to see their children somewhat better off than other people's children. So while, in the abstract, Andrew Carnegie had a case, I really would not want to be the politician who tried to enact his doctrine into rigorous law. Besides, it really would not be worth the bother. Inheritance of wealth is not a serious source of inequality in American society. Most people who have a very high income today have earned their money. For every Rockefeller there are a dozen popular singers, movie stars, outstanding athletes, clever entrepreneurs, etc.

We do have a most amusing paradox that has been revealed over the past ten years. Some persons in the academic community are terribly exercised about the issue of income inequality. As a consequence, some politicians have become terribly exercised about it, and they have tried to interest the American people in the subject. The American people always reply: "Cut our taxes, please. Don't tell me about raising someone else's taxes. I'm not interested in raising someone else's taxes. All I want you to do is cut my taxes." Senator McGovern, of course, discovered this at first hand. He had the very clever idea, invented at MIT by a brilliant young economist, of "reforming" the tax system so as to limit all private fortunes to $500,000. To his astonishment, the working class people he spoke to did not like that at all. They wanted a chance to make a million dollars, or they wanted their children to have the chance. They knew the odds were very much against it. On the other hand, they thought it made life more interesting to have the opportunity, whatever the odds.

The issue of equality keeps being propounded by academics and by some politicians. But it keeps being rejected by the American people, who in every poll show themselves to be profoundly indifferent to the subject. They are interested in improving their condition. They are not interested in taking punitive action against other people who have been especially successful in improving their condition. That is one reason our economic system works. After all, if the majority were interested in constantly punishing people who succeeded, we would have a system which encouraged people to make money and then punished them for making money—and that would not work at all.

My point is that if one wishes to understand the roots of that anti-capitalist sentiment so widely expressed today, one really has to ignore the more typical accusations that are leveled against the system. It is not for such reasons that people are opposed to or do not like the system. In order to understand what is at issue here, one has to look at our liberal democratic capitalist system from the other end of the telescope. Do not try to understand it from the perspective of 1978. Try to see it from the perspective of 1678. This is a very odd and exceptional economic, political, and social system we live in. We do not see how odd it is because it is ours, we were born and raised in it. We do not even perceive its distinctive features. Even those who oppose it often do not understand why they are opposing it.

Let me raise a question: Why did this system emerge only in the eighteenth century? Why did it not emerge in the fourteenth century? In pondering that question one begins to get a clue as to the source of anti-capitalist sentiment today. The reason capitalism did not emerge prior to the eighteenth century is because there were certain forces opposed to its emerging. Specifically, there were certain institutions and certain classes that did not want to see a capitalist economic sector develop. Business is not new, business was not invented by capitalism, and the notion that you could have more and more business taking place was not foreign to pre-capitalist social orders. But the institutions and the classes of those periods always saw the expansion of business—of commercial transactions between consenting adults—as a threat, and always constrained such transactions within narrow boundaries. The institutions and classes I am referring to include the church, the aristocracy, most of the learned class, certainly military castes. They opposed the expansion of the private commercial sector because they had certain ideals as to what a good society is, and they wanted to preserve for themselves the power to shape the civilization of that society. They did not want to relinquish that power to the market place. And, one must understand, that is precisely what happens under liberal capitalism, a capitalism operating under limited government.

The civilization of capitalism is shaped—not entirely, but to a considerable degree—by the market place. If people will pay fifty dollars to go see a football game, but will not pay twenty dollars to go to the opera, you have a successful football team and a less successful opera. If people do not want to build churches but want to build highways, you have a civilization with more highways and fewer churches. A capitalist economic system transfers to the market place that authority which used to reside in certain specific classes—the church, the clergy, the aristocracy—who claimed for themselves the right to define the shape of civilization for everyone.

Thus, in the Middle Ages we got beautiful cathedrals built by people who might have used that time to improve their own little huts and shanties. They were not given the choice. Granted, some of them might have volunteered to build those cathedrals, but I assume that a great many more would have said: "Thank you very much, I'll stay home and fix the roof which is leaking, and do something about the pig sty, from which the pig keeps escaping." In short, given the choice, they might have chosen to look after their own self-interests.

Further, in all precapitalist societies, giving such priority to one's own self-interest was thought to be wrong, even sinful. The church said it was wrong. The aristocracy said it was wrong. The monarchy said it was wrong. The learned men said it was wrong. When you have a civilization and a social order with a class of people who *know* what is right and what is wrong, and whose knowledge is power because they have the authority to enforce that knowledge, then obviously you cannot have a capitalist economic system.

Another thing we fail to see because we take the wrong historical perspective is that capitalism is decidedly an economic system for common men and common women. Capitalism panders to their major interests in life: themselves and their families and improving the circumstances of themselves and their families. Capitalism does not say to the average man, "The greatest glory you can have is to go and die on a battlefield for your country or your religion." And it does not say, "The greatest glory you can have is to become a devout, pious man whose life is an *imitatio Christi.*" It does not exclude those possibilities, and it gives you the right to do these things if you wish, but basically the values of a capitalist civilization are such that most ordinary people will spend most of their time and energies in improving their conditions and in enjoying the commonly-shared amenities.

Capitalism recognizes the legitimacy of self-interest as a moving force for the individual, and removes the moral stigma previously attached to it. But it is also taken for granted that a free people will set reasonable limits on and go beyond their self-interested activities. Self-interest is different from greed or avarice, which are by nature boundless. Capitalism has always taken for granted that human beings, once they have satisfied their self-interests to a certain degree, would indulge other interests such as religion, the arts, social activities, patriotism, and philanthropy. But these would be voluntary activities, involving no *compulsory* sacrifice of self-interest.

At issue in the world today is the question, Who is going to have the power to shape our civilization? We know who has the power in communist countries. The Party has the power. The Party claims the power for exactly the same reason that the Catholic Church claimed that power in the Middle Ages—because it believes it possesses authoritative knowledge of what is good for people. It consequently believes that what people say is good for them, or what they seem to prefer, is irrelevant. It *knows*. And if you have a class of people—whether it be an aristocracy or a clergy or a political party (which can be a kind of secularized clergy)—who can successfully establish their claim to authoritative knowledge, then you do not need a liberal society and you do not want a liberal society. If there is someone who knows what is best, what is the point of having people freely express their preferences and opinions? The sensible thing, then, is for everyone to listen to that one authoritative source of true wisdom.

Liberal capitalism is the first economic and social system in the history of the world which admits that no one really knows what is best. True, many people know some things, and some people know more than others, so deference is permissible. No one, however, can legitimately claim the authority that the Catholic Church claimed in the Middle Ages or the Communist Party claims in the Soviet Union today, or the aristocracy claimed in sixteenth-century France. No one can claim the authority to say, "This is—never mind what you want—this is what you need. We'll give you what you need, and what you want is irrelevant." Capitalism says, "What you want is relevant. You can take guidance, if you wish. You can be instructed, if you wish, by people whom you think to be wiser or more learned than you. But, in the end, you decide. You decide in the market place by spending your money. You can give all your money to the church—there is nothing to stop you. On the other hand, if you want to buy an automobile, that is your privilege." In the Soviet Union, the ruling Party wants few privately-owned automobiles. Of course the ordinary people in the Soviet Union do want them, but never mind, the Party has decided that they do not need them, that it is bad for them to have automobiles. And the Party can say this in good conscience because it believes it knows the truth.

As I noted earlier, liberal capitalism is in some ways a quite "vulgar" system. It is the only economic and social system in the world's history which says, "Look, the common aspirations of ordinary men and women are to be respected. Their self-interest is legitimate. Any idea of 'the common good' must be congruent with that self-interest. No one has the right simply to impose an idea of the common good on them." The consequence is a society that is at least as contented as any other and unquestionably far more prosperous, but also a society that does not satisfy those who feel they know, absolutely, what is right and what society should look like.

The world today seems to be producing more and more people—some learned, most merely schooled—who are certain they know what shape society should have and who do not want to leave this matter to be settled by free economic transactions between consenting adults. Some of these are people who really still think of themselves as "liberal," even as "democrats," because they have the interests of the people at heart. They believe the people do not know what is good for them and so they must tell them what is good for them. The environmentalist movement, the ecological movement, the movement for more government regulation and centralized economic planning—the emergence of such trends indicates how powerful this urge is to tell other people how to lead their lives, for their own good of course.

George Will has made a most useful distinction between the New Deal kind of liberalism and this new kind of liberalism. The older liberalism, he says, wanted the government to intervene so as to help people live the way they wanted to live; the new liberalism wants to tell people how to live. This new liberalism is not interested in making people able to buy their own automobiles, if they want them. It wants to tell them whether or not they can buy automobiles, what kind of automobiles to buy, where they may park them, where they may drive in the city, and many other things besides.

What we are really talking about is a resurgence in our own

lifetime, and most especially within the past twenty years, of the very ancient notion that there is a party, a class, a group of people who have authoritative political knowledge and who can, using this knowledge, achieve something called "social justice." They know what the "right" division of income should be, they know who should and should not be rewarded. They know who should get rich and who should not be permitted to get rich. They know who should be honored and who should not. They *know,* and they are itching to impose their knowledge on the American people. Theirs is a most self-righteous hunger for power.

We are, in other words, witnessing in our own age an historic reversion to a precapitalist mode of thinking among large numbers of people. For the most part, these are our college-educated thinkers. It is most natural, if you have spent many years in school and have a certificate testifying that you are now a learned person, to feel that this puts you in a different class from those who did not go to college. You must know more than they do; therefore, your opinion should count for more than theirs. With the post-World War II upsurge of mass higher education in the United States, Britain, France, Germany, Italy, and elsewhere, we have produced a very large number of people who have a natural instinct for assuming authority.

What makes this class as powerful as it is and gives it such a popular base, however, is the element of "utopianism" in modern thought. After all, why would anyone give this class the authority which it feels it has a right to? Why, especially, should ordinary people do it? Are they completely gullible? No, I do not think they are gullible. The reason for the influence of this "new class" is that we live in a world shot through with utopian secular longings, utopian secular yearnings. These longings and yearnings were once encompassed, "contained" as it were, by religion. It has always been religion which assures people that, though their lives may seem meaningless, there is meaning to them nevertheless which will one day be revealed. Religion also offers the assurance that the evident injustices of the world will somehow be compensated for in the long run, so it will all make moral sense. When religion loses its appeal and persuasiveness, as has certainly been the case during this century, all the "unfairnesses" of life, all its limitations, are felt as more and more intolerable. People then demand that "someone" do something about it, and that "someone" is inevitably the politician. What the churches once promised for the vague future, government now promises in the here and now. Politicians with authoritative answers find their congregations swelling.

More and more people today are also becoming convinced that government has what used to be called "the healing touch." The medieval king was supposedly able to cure leprosy by touching the victim. Now, more and more people look to central government as the healer of society's problems. If something is wrong, one need only go to government, and government will provide a solution. But, of course, to think that the world consists of something called "problems" to which there are corresponding "solutions" is to misunderstand the nature of reality. Yes, there are some problems in the world, to which there are some solutions, but most of the afflictions we call "problems" are more properly described as conditions to be coped with as best one can. The very use of the terms "problems" and "solutions" indicates the kind of utopian rationalism which suffuses the modern political imagination.

And so we are experiencing a tremor of spiritual restlessness moving among the people, affecting all of them to one degree or another. This is not because capitalism fails to deliver on its promises. It is, rather, because capitalism does not promise very much from a utopian perspective. All it promises is that people will be able to better their condition and that they will have a great deal of liberty as they do so. That is all, and it is not much. Most political systems promise, and have always promised, much, much more. Once there is a decline of religion, therefore, capitalism is very vulnerable to political movements and their promises of utopia.

Now, I do not want to appear too pessimistic. Liberal capitalism is in deep trouble, but it has sturdy roots in reality that are not easily destroyed. Meanwhile, all over the world utopian ideas are being discredited in their turn, as they give birth to political systems that range from the hideous to the merely squalid. Anticapitalism has had its victories. There are now plenty of communist, socialist, or quasi-socialist nations. But do we observe that any one of them is pointed out to us as a model to emulate? No, it is always imaginary societies whose virtues are celebrated, as contrasted with liberal capitalism. And one would like to think that a preference for pie-in-the-sky, as against home-made (or even packaged) apple pie, cannot by its nature endure.

Still, I believe that a revival of religion is an absolute precondition for the preservation of common sense in this country. That may sound paradoxical, but it is not really. There has to be a sphere in which all the injustices and painful limitations of this world are rectified; and it should be beyond the reach of politics. If one sets out to correct all the injustices of the world, someone will soon claim the need for absolute power to do it—the power to define injustice, to act upon a particular conception of injustice, to remove the evil once and for all. And we end up with a society which authoritatively declares itself to be a just society—and which silences all those who think otherwise.

FOUR

National Regulation

of the

International Economy:

A Business Perspective

Mark Shepherd, Jr.

Chairman, Chief Executive Officer
Texas Instruments Incorporated

Since World War II, most of the Free World nations have shared a common commitment to an increasingly open international economic order. Now this commitment has been challenged on three fronts:

1. Protectionist measures have been increasingly adopted to restrict product imports to protect domestic industries and jobs.
2. Pressures are mounting to restrict technology outflows to prevent the export of jobs.
3. Many governments now are demanding access to technology as a condition for foreign investment or market entry in order to achieve national goals for technology advancement and modernization.

All three of these trends are interrelated and reflect a loss of confidence that the private sector can best make the decisions affecting the flow of products, capital, and technology among Free World nations. These trends have affected relations among the industrialized nations, as well as relations between developed and developing nations.

This chapter argues that the trend toward greater government regulation represents a short-term and short-sighted response to more fundamental economic issues confronting all nations. It examines the underlying causes for the turn toward greater government regulation, and offers some suggestions that would help individual nations to pursue their national economic goals without resorting to greater governmental controls.

Some Definitions. Trade, technology transfer, and foreign investment have been used imprecisely in the current debates. Trade refers to the flow of products between nations. Technology has implied everything from basic research to technical education to the actual machines that perform a manufacturing operation, and even to finished products. As it is used in this chapter, technology is industrial know-how. It is the application of specialized and technical knowledge to the creation of a new and useful product, or to the performance of a specific task. It encompasses the thousands of detailed steps that are necessary to develop, manufacture, and market a product. It is generally the private property of individual firms.

A similar confusion exists over the distinction between technology transfer and foreign investment. Technology transfer has been used to characterize the movement of products, capital, and know-how between nations. "Transfers" can occur in many ways, but for our purposes the term refers to those in which control and ownership are relinquished or shared, that is, through joint ventures, co-production, or outright sales of know-how. This is distinct from foreign direct investment, where the transferring party retains control and ownership of the technology.

THE INDUSTRIALIZED NATIONS

The pressures for more government regulation among industrialized nations have come during a period of slower economic growth, high inflation, changes in relative competitive strength, and a large oil debt, problems which have plagued all industrialized nations of the Free World. Since these problems are structural, not cyclical in nature, they likely will remain for the foreseeable future.

Figure 4.1 shows the pattern of Gross National Product (GNP)

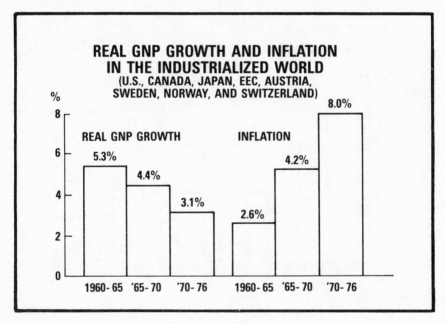

Figure 4.1

growth and consumer prices for the industrialized world in three different time periods. Between 1960 and 1965, the industrial countries of the world grew at an average of 5.3 percent per year. Measured from 1970 to 1976, this growth rate was only 3.1 percent. Conversely, inflation has risen from 2.6 percent in the 1960–65 time frame to 8.0 percent in the 1970–76 period.

The relative economic strength among the developed nations has changed as Japan's economy has grown more rapidly than that of either the U.S. or the European Economic Community (Figure 4.2). Despite its well-known liabilities, high population density and a scarcity of raw materials and energy sources, Japan's average annual real GNP growth rate was more than 10 percent per year between 1960 and 1970, compared with rates of under 5 percent for the U.S. and the European Economic Community. During 1970–76, Japan managed to keep its annual growth at more than 5 percent, while the U.S. and the European Economic Community grew at less than 3 percent.

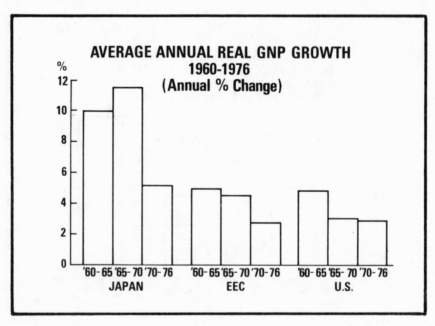

Figure 4.2

As a result of Japan's success in the export of manufactured goods, the U.S. trade deficit with Japan grew to $8.1 billion in 1977, and the EEC trade deficit with Japan grew to about $5 billion.[1] Certain market segments, such as steel, consumer electronics, autos, and shipbuilding, have been hit particularly hard.

The massive transfer of capital from oil importing to oil exporting nations is responsible for some of these trends (Figure 4.3).

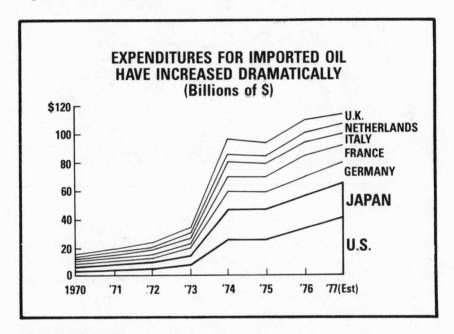

Figure 4.3

Between 1973 and 1977, the Free World's major oil consuming nations have paid more than $400 billion for imported oil. About half of this has been paid by the U.S. and Japan. These disruptions have cost the U.S. $60 billion in real Gross National Product in 1976 alone, amounting to $600 per working person in real income.[2] The relative impact of oil imports on the U.S. is even greater than these numbers suggest.

Figure 4.4 shows that the real delivered price of OPEC benchmark crude actually has declined for every major importer since its

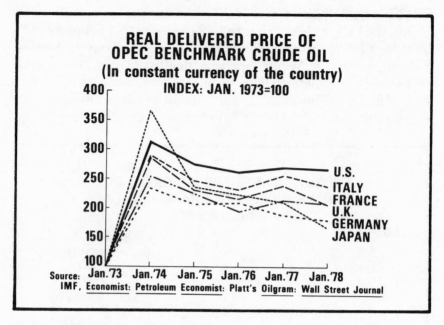

Figure 4.4

initial jump in October 1973. The reason for the decline is inflation and the weakness of the U.S. dollar. Note that OPEC oil being priced in dollar terms, coupled with the deteriorating exchange rate of the dollar, resulted in a less pronounced real price decline for the U.S. than for other industrialized countries.

The oil price hike has heightened the sense of vulnerability of oil importing nations and has led all except the U.S. to seek all possible alternative energy sources for the future.

The United States

In the U.S., barriers to trade have been emerging, directed primarily against selected Japanese industries such as steel and consumer electronics products. In addition, barriers have emerged to the import of sugar, textiles, and several other products of developing nations which have threatened domestic industries and jobs. Although no legislation has been adopted, pressures to restrict capital and technology outflows also are mounting, among U.S. labor interests and some members of Congress, to preserve jobs and protect a declining U.S. technological leadership position.

Despite the protectionist pressures brought about by these changing global conditions, the U.S. must resist the temptation to erect barriers to trade inflows and to capital and technology outflows. Such government regulation will invite retaliation from other countries, and although protecting jobs in the short term, actually could reduce U.S. job opportunities in the long term.

In particular, the government clearly must not start down a path toward restricting those overseas ventures in which multinational corporations retain control of the technology. Multinational corporations invest overseas either to gain better access to markets or to reduce manufacturing costs. In either case the motive is growth, which in turn creates jobs at home as well as overseas.

Costs, and prices in turn, decline at a predictable rate with accumulated volume. It follows that a company that participates in a total world market has an inherent economic advantage over a company confined to building its production base on a national market only.

If a company were forced to manufacture in only a single country, it might soon find itself noncompetitive and either out of business or subsidized by the government. By establishing a network of overseas subsidiaries, Texas Instruments, for example, has both expanded its markets and reduced its costs. These are crucial to survival in the highly competitive electronics industry. As a result, our employment has grown both in the U.S. and overseas.

It is more controversial for U.S. firms to sell technology to foreign competitors because this may improve the international competitive position of these firms. Nonetheless, government regulation of technology exports based on economic considerations is not the answer. Although export controls for military purposes should continue, governments simply do not have the capability to determine the net economic costs and benefits to a nation from technology exports. It is best left to individual firms that hopefully will exercise a strategic regard for technology as a matter of self-preservation.

Improved Productivity. Greater government regulation will not solve our underlying problem in the U.S., which is the low rate of productivity growth. Slower economic growth, rapid inflation, and a decreased competitive position are merely the symptoms. The U.S. simply is consuming more, dedicating a declining percentage of resources to research and development, and investing less.

Productivity improvement is the driving force of the noninflationary economic growth that increases our living standards. As shown in Figure 4.5, Japan's real Gross National Product grew at 8.8 percent per year between 1960 and 1976 on the strength of annual productivity gains of about 8 percent. On the other hand, the U.S. and the U.K., with productivity gains close to 2 percent, experienced annual real GNP growth of only about 3 percent.

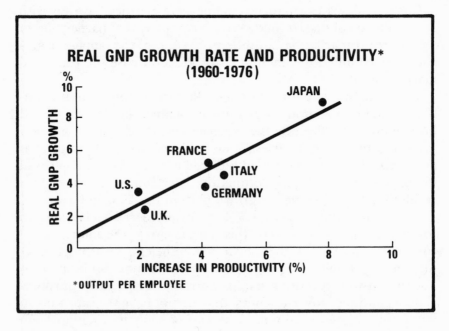

Figure 4.5

Despite the recent low level of productivity increase in the U.S., the strong performance of the U.S. economy historically has enabled it to achieve high absolute levels of productivity compared with other countries.

Economic research by Edward Denison at Brookings,[3] among others, indicates that almost one-half of the U.S. increase in productivity for the last 30 years is attributable to technological innovation (Figure 4.6). Technological change interacts with, and is embodied in, new capital goods. However, it is a distinct process and one that often can be capital-saving rather than capital-using.

Research and development is the backbone of innovation, and the same relationship that exists between productivity and real GNP growth also exists between R&D expenditures and real GNP growth. Figure 4.7 shows that those countries with higher rates of growth in R&D expenditures also have higher GNP growth rates. Japan, with an average increase in R&D expenditures of 18.7

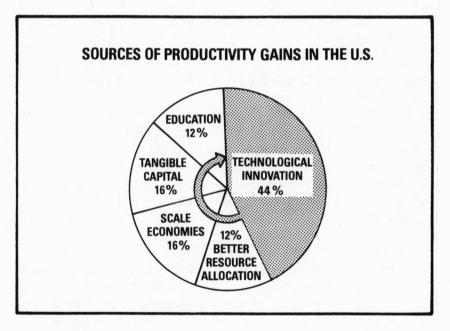

Figure 4.6

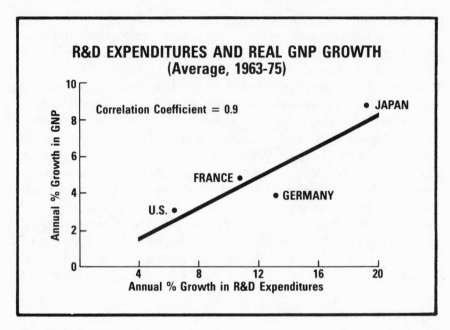

Figure 4.7

percent, had the highest real GNP growth rate of 8.5 percent. The U.S., with an average increase in R&D expenditures of 6.2 percent, had a GNP growth rate of 3 percent over the time period 1963–75.

Although increasing in absolute terms, the decline since 1964 in U.S. R&D expenditures as a percentage of Gross National Product (Figure 4.8) is reason for concern. The two major European countries, Germany and France, also have experienced declines in the more recent past. On the other hand, Japan, except for a 1975 dip, has been steadily increasing its R&D effort and is likely to become a major developer of technology in the future.

Along with food, high-technology products have been the most important U.S. export items. This means Japan poses an even greater problem in the future to the U.S. balance of trade.

Gains in productivity also follow increases in investment in tangible capital. The chart at the left of Figure 4.9 indicates that

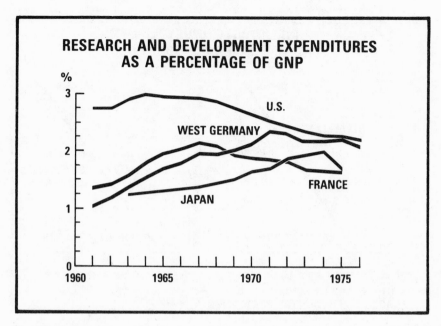

Figure 4.8

countries with a higher proportion of GNP devoted to total investment also have higher productivity increases. Japan, investing 33
percent of GNP, had productivity growth close to 9 percent. Most
countries in Western Europe invested close to 20 percent of GNP
and their productivity gains averaged about 5 percent. Productivity
growth in the U.S. hovered between 2 percent and 3 percent, with
less than 15 percent of GNP allocated to investment.

The chart at the right of Figure 4.9 confirms one of the cor-
nerstones of the free enterprise system. Countries with higher
investment expenditures have higher GNP growth rates. It is real
GNP growth that creates employment opportunities and increases
living standards. Capital investment, however, has been and will
continue to be a problem.

One reason is a high level of government spending. If we
exclude transfer payments, the U.S., with the highest level of

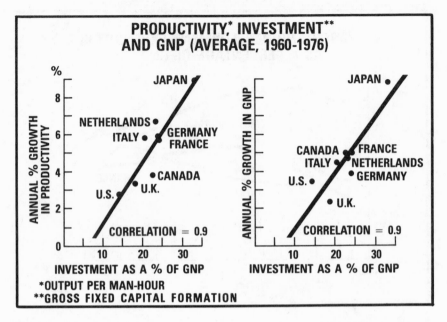

Figure 4.9

government spending as a percent of GNP, also has the lowest level of investment as a percentage of GNP among major industrialized nations. This is because government borrowing, along with a corporate tax structure that gives the government a 50 percent equity ownership with zero investment, simply takes away resources that would have financed expenditures for capital goods. Thus, as seen in a matrix for major industrialized countries, public spending comes at the expense of capital investment and this process deprives the economy of a major source of productivity growth (Figure 4.10).

Figure 4.11 demonstrates the problem of funding growth. It depicts the relationship between asset turnover and return on assets within the total U.S. manufacturing sector, which determines, in turn, the rate of sales growth that can be funded by the manufacturing industry from its cash flow. Note that on average

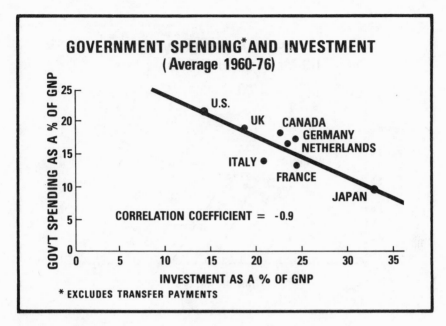

GOVERNMENT SPENDING*AND INVESTMENT
(Average 1960-76)

GOV'T SPENDING AS A % OF GNP

U.S.

UK   CANADA
      GERMANY
      NETHERLANDS

ITALY ●

FRANCE

JAPAN

CORRELATION COEFFICIENT = -0.9

INVESTMENT AS A % OF GNP

* EXCLUDES TRANSFER PAYMENTS

Figure 4.10

for the 1970–76 time period, profitability was sufficient to self-fund an average annual sales growth of 7 percent, a rate that barely exceeded that period's average annual rate of inflation of 6 percent.

If performance remains at the 1974 level during the period 1977–85, the manufacturing sector could self-fund an average annual sales growth of 9 percent. If, however, the level of profitability slips back to the 1970–76 average, funding the same 9 percent sales growth would require additional external capital of almost one-quarter of a trillion dollars.

If we assume just a one-percentage-point increase in inflation to 7 percent, which adjusts the growth rate of sales upward by an equal amount but does not affect other variables, the external capital requirement for the 1974 example would be raised by roughly $85 billion. This does not include the problem inflation

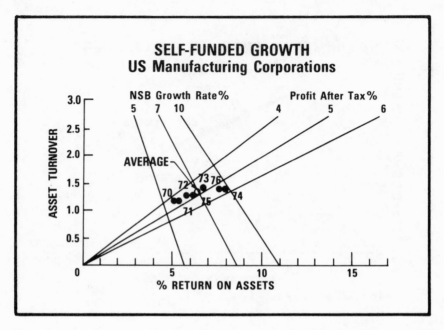

Figure 4.11

creates by increasing both the taxes on the existing capital stock and the replacement costs for capital. However, if inflation were at the historical rate of slightly over 3 percent, then under the same assumptions, there would be no external capital requirements.

Moreover, limitations on the availability of balance sheet data restricted this analysis to the manufacturing sector. The omission of heavy users of capital, such as the utilities and communications industries, implies external capital requirements will be much greater for the total economy. According to a study by the New York Stock Exchange, the estimated savings potential through 1985 of just over $4 trillion will fall short of accumulated demand, creating a capital gap of about $650 billion.

There are potential problems of future capital supply, which will make such external requirements difficult to meet. Continued high inflation will move people with level or decreasing real incomes into higher tax brackets, which decreases their ability to save. A study recently published by the National Bureau of Economic Research[4] argues that increases in Social Security benefits lead to almost equal dollar reductions in retirement nest eggs. Therefore, a lot less money becomes available for capital investment.

An Agenda for U.S. Action. It follows that in order to remain competitive, and at the same time avoid a capital shortage, U.S. policies must be changed to stimulate capital formation and R&D expenditures.

Lowering corporate and personal tax rates, increasing the investment tax credit, eliminating the double taxation of dividends, and permitting more rapid depreciation of production equipment and facilities would allow the business community to formulate optimal long-term investment plans.

Also, a tax credit for research and development expenditures not only would free corporate funds for investment purposes, but also would channel funds to high-technology industries with heavy R&D expenditures—businesses that can make the greatest contribution in stimulating the economy, increasing employment, and reducing inflation.

As an alternative, a substantial corporate tax rate cut, accompanied by a decrease in the money supply and in government expenditures—all planned over five to seven years—would free corporate funds for investment and R&D expenditures. This, in turn, would reduce inflation and produce jobs.

The U.S., however, cannot do it alone. Other industrialized nations also must adopt measures to stimulate their economies and develop technologies within an open international system.

Western Europe

In Europe, intense protectionist sentiments have developed against a wide range of Japanese products—from steel and ball bearings, to television and automobiles. A continued decline of the dollar is likely to intensify protectionist pressures against U.S. products.

Despite its outstanding performance in the decades of the fifties and the sixties, European industry has faced, in the past few years, major structural problems that remain unresolved. These problems are centered around increasing costs, stronger competition from overseas, and declining rates of productivity improvement. Labor is reluctant to accept automation, management is tolerant of underemployment on the job, and unemployment benefits are approaching full wage levels.

It is not only the U.S. that is suffering a bout of underinvestment. With deteriorating profit margins, Europe is also losing its attraction for new investment capital. After several years of world economic recovery, there still is no sign of any dramatic pickup in private capital spending, and there are indications that investment outlays may stagnate for at least the rest of the decade.

One of the major problems is that Europe is well into the age of state capitalism. The shaded sections in Figure 4.12 show the per-

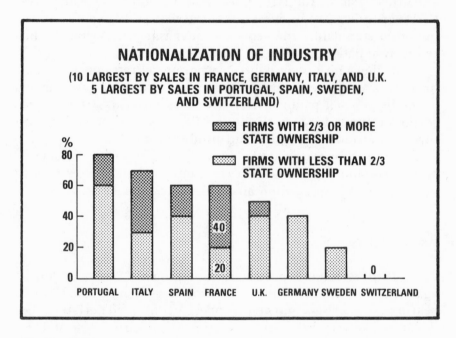

Figure 4.12

centage of the ten largest firms in each country that are at least two-thirds government-owned. In France, for example, the government owns at least two-thirds of two of the ten largest companies. The government owns a smaller share in another four of the ten.

State-owned corporations are viewed by their governments as social institutions whose purpose is to provide jobs rather than to earn profits in a competitive environment. They will not be allowed to fail regardless of how inefficient they are. This produces a drag on the economy for which the shrinking private sector must compensate.

Wage increases in Europe are exceeding gains in productivity by wide margins, and during 1970–76, hourly compensation increased at an average annual rate of 16.5 percent, compared with 8.0 percent for the United States (Figure 4.13). As a result, unit

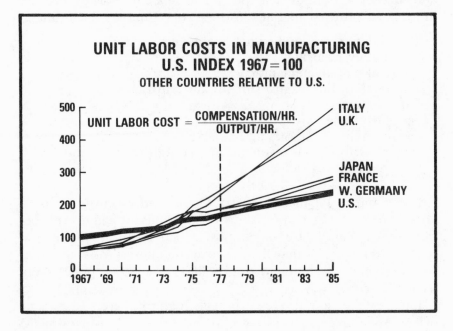

Figure 4.13

labor costs have increased twice as fast in Europe as in the U.S., making European goods less competitive in international markets. As shown in the plot, in 1977 the U.S. had absolute unit labor costs lower than all major industrialized countries except France.

For European industry—particularly Italy and the U.K.—to be competitive, wage increases must be kept in line with productivity increases. A reduced level of governmental intervention in domestic industry also would help. Government is an inefficient manager and does not provide the rewards for efficiency that spur productivity.

Japan

Many of the reasons for the chronic U.S. and European trade and current account deficits with Japan relate to basic differences in the way industry operates in these two countries, including:

The ability to respond to national goals;
Debt-equity ratios;
National employment practices;
The relationship of government and industry;
Capital supply;
Social overhead costs;
Composition of imports and exports;
Impact of foreign investment on trading practices; and
National export orientation.

For example, Japanese industry focuses more heavily on long-term market share than on short-term profits. It can do this because of higher debt-equity ratios, which means that the first concern of many Japanese firms is covering interest costs with their banks. Profits, dividends to stockholders, and stock prices are a secondary concern.

Japanese industry also has especially high fixed costs because of heavy capital expenditures (and, in some areas, over-investment) and their lifetime employment system. During periods of economic slowdown, high fixed costs pressure Japanese firms to increase exports on the basis of incremental prices in international markets. This leads to charges of dumping by other countries.

Since many of these differences are ingrained in social and cultural patterns, they resist ready change. They must be properly understood to be dealt with, and solutions will be difficult and long-term.

In the short term, Japan's most immediate challenge is not one of competitiveness, but one of opening its economy to trade and foreign investment from the U.S. and Europe. This is difficult politically for Japan, which faces strong internal pressures to protect domestic industries and jobs.

As Figure 4.14 illustrates, when Japan's economy was weaker, the U.S. did not pressure the Japanese to open their economy to outside trade and investment. In 1960, only 1 percent of total U.S.

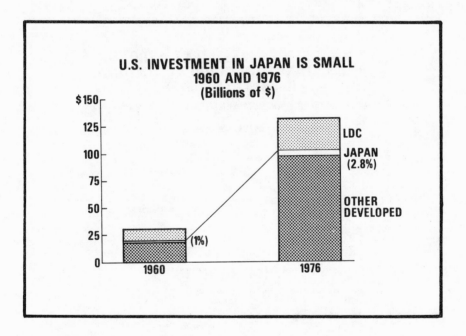

Figure 4.14

foreign investment was in Japan. Although pressures from the U.S. have mounted, the percentage of U.S. investment in Japan was only 2.8 percent in 1976. This is very small, and from our own experience at Texas Instruments we know that achieving a completely U.S.-owned subsidiary in Japan is a long and arduous process.

Many critics will argue that a greater outflow of capital to Japan would hurt, rather than help, our balance-on-current-account situation with Japan.

As Figure 4.15 shows, the larger the level of U.S. foreign direct investment in a particular country or region, the more favorable the balance. U.S. firms tend to lack an export orientation because of our large domestic market and the provincialism of the average U.S. citizen. As a result, U.S. firms tend to trade most heavily with those countries in which they have their greatest manufacturing

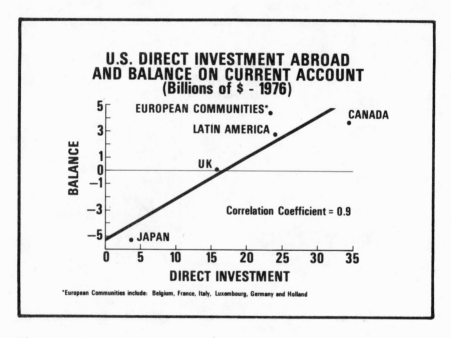

Figure 4.15

investment. A higher level of U.S. investment in Japan would have the "pull-through" effect of increasing U.S. exports.

In summary, measures to increase government regulation of trade, investment, and technology transfer among developed countries are precisely the wrong steps. What is needed in Europe and the U.S. is less, not more, government intervention in private enterprise, and positive incentives for capital formation and innovation. Japan must reduce its barriers to trade and investment in keeping with its role as a major economic power.

DEVELOPING NATIONS

Technology transfer has been a central issue in the North-South dialogue. Many less-developed countries, or LDCs, believe the multinational corporation works counter to their modernization goals, and they have adopted laws to regulate more heavily the flow of technology and foreign investment into their countries.

The primary focus of LDC efforts has been to improve the quality of, cost of, and conditions for receiving technology. They feel in particular that the multinational corporations have been insensitive to their needs in refusing to relinquish technology to them.

The initiatives of individual nations have been reinforced by the United Nations. The Code of Conduct proposed by the United Nations Committee on Trade and Development represents an attempt to provide sanction under international law for nations to:

Increase regulation of patent protection;

Decrease control by the supplier over the protection and use of his technology;

Impose more limitations on contracts between supplier and user; and

Reduce payments when technology is purchased.

The problem with this approach is that it may reduce, not increase, LDC access to technology, and may deprive LDCs of the other benefits of foreign direct investment.

Technology is Private Property. The fundamental problem with the political demand of developing nations for access to technology is that know-how generally is owned by private companies, not by governments, and it must be transferred under conditions that respect the rights of ownership and control by prospective suppliers.

There is a second and related problem: In general, companies do not develop technology to sell, but to make products to sell in the world marketplace. It is the difference between selling the cotton crop and selling the farm. The engine of risk and reward drives technology development. Firms respond to forcing functions such as the requirement for productivity improvement, personal needs, energy conservation and management, and national defense. They invest in technology because they expect it will lead to a profit for the company.

Texas Instruments has acquired its technological leadership in the semiconductor industry at high risk, high cost, and great effort by its scientists and engineers. It uses financial resources made available by individuals and institutions investing in the company. These investors expect and are entitled to a fair return on their investment.

The value placed on technology varies across corporations. Some firms, particularly those using more mature technologies, have policies that permit both the sale of technology and joint ownership and control. Other corporations, primarily in high-technology areas, may be unwilling to turn over control of their most sophisticated technologies as a condition for transfer. Texas Instruments, for example, has established a policy of total TI ownership and control of overseas plants. Further, TI does not sell semiconductor and other advanced technologies for use by others.

For us, the only adequate payment for technology is market share. Without an opportunity to share in the market served, or without adequate protection of one's proprietary technological position, there would be little or no incentive to risk the investment needed to develop an innovative technology. And certainly there would be no incentive to transfer it to someone else.

Ability to Absorb Technology. Even if multinational firms agree to sell or relinquish some control over their technology, developing countries cannot absorb and effectively utilize it unless they have the infrastructure of scientists, engineers and managers; local sources of supply of materials and components for finished products; and a work force capable of learning the necessary skills.

Industrial know-how is often complex, beginning as an idea, but including market analysis, engineering design, new manufacturing processes, prototyping, pilot production, testing, quality control, and distribution to the customer (Figure 4.16). It includes the

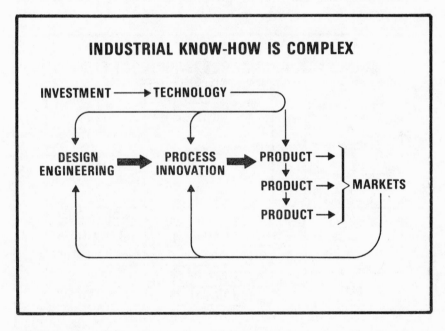

Figure 4.16

additional engineering work and process innovations that continue throughout a product's lifetime to improve its performance and reduce its cost.

To illustrate the complexity of industrial know-how, let me draw an example again from Texas Instruments (Figure 4.17). In the first phase of manufacturing integrated circuits, very pure silicon crystals must be grown and sawed into slices. Circuitry is designed with the aid of a computer. A photolithographic process is used to transfer an image of the circuitry onto the slice. One slice may contain hundreds or thousands of individual integrated circuit chips, and each chip may, in turn, contain thousands of individual components. Because of the sophistication of the technology there is a need to maintain close contact with the research, development, and design engineering operations of the corporation. This phase of the process, therefore, is carried out in the U.S., Western

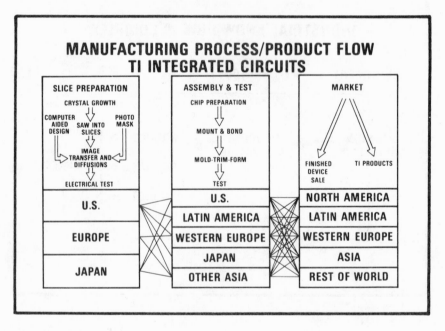

Figure 4.17

Europe, and Japan, where the needed scientists and engineers are readily available.

In the second phase of the process, the individual chips are assembled into semiconductor components and tested. This phase of our process is conducted in our manufacturing facilities in the U.S., Latin America, Western Europe, Japan, and other Asian countries.

These components then are marketed in the U.S., Japan, Europe, and the rest of the world, and also are used in many TI products such as watches, calculators, and minicomputers.

Impact on Foreign Investment. By emphasizing access to technology, LDCs may discourage foreign investment. Many of the LDCs argue as if they can count on attracting multinational investment regardless of their laws and regulations. In fact multinational investment is spread around the world, and each decision to invest is made very carefully. Investment grows in countries and regions where favorable political, economic, and social conditions exist.

As shown in Figure 4.18, between 1966 and 1976 U.S. direct investment abroad increased at an average annual rate of about 10 percent.[5] The bulk of this investment was in developed countries—about 68 percent in 1966, and almost 74 percent in 1976. Investment in developing countries is increasing, but at an average annual rate of only 7.7 percent.

Latin America has been the recipient of more than one-half of U.S. investment in developing countries, although in recent years the greatest growth in U.S. investment has been in the Caribbean and in Asia.[6]

Some of the developing nations argue as though they believe multinational investment impedes economic development. In responding to this, it is important to distinguish between natural-resource-oriented and manufacturing-oriented multinational corporations. The former are draining off wealth that is exhaustible; the latter are creating wealth and skills that are not exhaustible, but regenerative.

Increasingly, U.S. multinational investment in LDCs has been in manufacturing, and not extractive industries. Between 1966 and

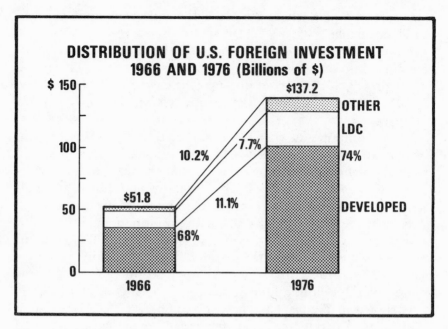

Figure 4.18

1976 manufacturing investment has grown from $3.5 billion to $11.4 billion, or an average annual growth rate of 12.4 percent (Figure 4.19). As a percentage of total U.S. investment in LDCs, manufacturing investment has grown from about 25 percent to over 39 percent.

Benefits of Multinationals to LDCs. A manufacturing-oriented corporation can choose to protect its technology, and still provide important benefits to the host country.

An obvious benefit has been to provide the LDCs with important sources of exports. Figure 4.20 examines a cross section of fifteen LDCs from Asia, Latin America, and Africa. Spain is also included in the analysis.[7] As the chart at the left of Figure 4.20 shows, the higher the level of new foreign direct investment, the higher the level of manufactured goods exported from the developing coun-

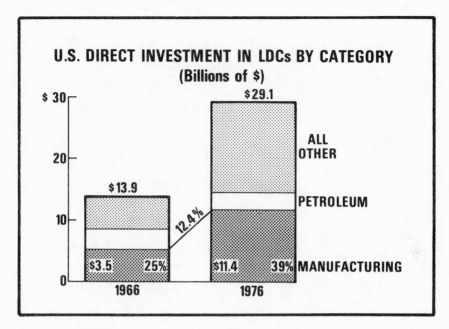

Figure 4.19

try. The chart at the right of Figure 4.20 shows that increasing their level of manufactured goods exports has increased their rate of economic growth. These relationships are particularly true for Korea, Taiwan, and Singapore, which have successfully attracted high levels of manufacturing investment and have also experienced rapid economic growth.

TI's experience with investments in Latin America and in Asia illustrates the infrastructure development provided by manufacturing-oriented foreign investment.

Each new TI plant established in these areas brought to the employees of the host country experience in sophisticated production technology, complex machinery, highly refined production planning, management, financial control systems similar to those used throughout the world, and a large import-export business.

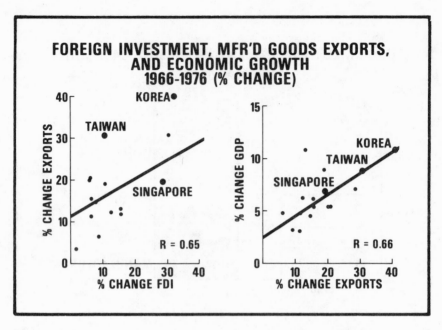

Figure 4.20

In addition to the intellectual expansion of host-country workers, these plants quickly generated:

Employment opportunities for both unskilled and skilled workers, including university-trained engineers;

Training opportunities, since the objective has been to staff each of the plants as much as possible with local nationals, including supervisory personnel, and to encourage advancement and promotion from within;

Local sourcing of supplies and raw materials to the extent possible; and

Increased exports from the LDC.

Closing the Economic Gap. Developing nations have placed great emphasis on closing the gap in economic well-being with developed nations. Closing the gap, however, will be extremely difficult. At this writing, the per capita GNP in developing countries is about $550. In developed countries it is about $6000. The gap, therefore, is about $5500.

As Figure 4.21 illustrates, if developed and developing nations both grow at 2.5 percent per year, the gap will widen to $8154 by the year 2000. A 5 percent real growth rate per year will mean a per capita income of only $618 in the year 2000 for LDCs, while developed nations would have a per capita GNP of more than $16,000. Even if the developed nations experienced no real economic growth; and developing nations experienced 10 percent real growth per year, the $1890 per capita GNP of LDCs in the year 2000 would be slightly more than one-half that of developed nations at $3220.

Importance of the Market System. Evidence indicates that the market

GNP PER CAPITA IN THE YEAR 2000 AT VARIOUS GROWTH RATES (1976 DOLLARS)

ANNUAL REAL GROWTH (%)	DEVELOPING NATIONS	DEVELOPED NATIONS	GAP
0%	$ 192	$ 3,220	$ 3,028
2.5	347	8,501	8,154
5	618	16,398	15,780
7.5	1,088	26,662	25,574
10	1,890	46,293	44,403

Figure 4.21

system is likely to do a better job than governments in making the economic decisions affecting capital investment and technology transfer.

To make this argument, let us compare the performance of countries traditionally classified as socialist with those that are capitalist, focusing on the extent of economic controls and state ownership. Some of them are dictatorships but still use the capitalist system. This analysis covers 70 percent of the people in the resource-rich Third World and resource-poor Fourth World nations.

The success of the capitalist system in the Fourth World countries is shown by comparing the per capita GNP growth during the period 1965–73 (Figure 4.22). During this time frame, each of the capitalist-oriented LDCs boasted a per capita GNP growth rate of 3 percent or better. In contrast, for the socialist group, no country

PER CAPITA REAL GNP GROWTH
FOURTH WORLD NATIONS
1965-1973

SOCIALISTIC (701 MILLION PEOPLE)		CAPITALISTIC (31 MILLION PEOPLE)	
AFGHANISTAN	0.9%	BOTSWANA	6.4%
BURMA	0.7	CAMEROON	4.9
CHAD	-3.3	CAPE VERDE ISLAND	6.0
GHANA	0.8	KENYA	3.3
GUINEA	0.1	MALAWI	3.7
GUYANA	1.1	GUINEA/BISSAU	5.9
INDIA	1.5	IVORY COAST	3.0
SUDAN	-0.6		
AVERAGE (0.2)		AVERAGE (4.7)	

Figure 4.22

had a growth rate above 1.5 percent, and real growth was negligible for the group as a whole.

The Third World economies build even a stronger case. The average growth rate for the capitalist countries was 6.2 percent, compared with 0.9 percent for the socialist nations (Figure 4.23). The socialist model of development just has not worked for them. It is surprising that, in spite of socialism's failure, we have been unable to "sell" our capitalist system to more countries. To make the problem even more serious, six times as many people still live in socialist LDCs as in capitalist ones.

LDC Priorities. Within a free market concept, developing nations need to establish national priorities that recognize the necessary balance and proper time phasing among all elements of the development process. Each LDC needs to understand what technologies are appropriate to the needs and resources of the country

PER CAPITA REAL GNP GROWTH
THIRD WORLD NATIONS
1965-1973

SOCIALISTIC (881 MILLION PEOPLE)		CAPITALISTIC (217 MILLION PEOPLE)	
CHILE	1.4 %	BARBADOS	5.8 %
CHINA, PEOPLE'S REPUBLIC	4.6	BRAZIL	6.0
CONGO, PEOPLE'S REPUBLIC	1.9	CHINA (TAIWAN)	7.3
CUBA	-0.7	HONG KONG	5.8
EQUATORIAL GUINEA	-3.1	KOREA, REPUBLIC OF	8.7
KOREA, DEMOCRATIC REP.	0.7	LIBERIA	4.7
MAURITIUS	1.4	SINGAPORE	9.4
PERU	1.8	RHODESIA	3.5
ZAMBIA	-0.2	CYPRUS	6.5
		THAILAND	4.5
AVERAGE	(0.9)	AVERAGE	(6.2)

Figure 4.23

and must attend to the educational, technological, and managerial infrastructure to be able to absorb the technology.

First, LDCs must do more to improve agricultural productivity
and distribution so they can feed themselves. Developed nations, as
a group, have produced 3.5 to 4 times as much grain per capita as
LDCs in the 1960s and 1970s. There are several reasons: good land
utilization; new technologies such as pesticides, fertilizers, her-
bicides, and mechanization; and available financing for the farmer.
As a result, the U.S. and Canada have become breadbaskets for the
world. Latin America, Africa, and Asia have become net importers
of grain (Figure 4.24). If developing nations could increase their
output per capita on the average by about 25 percent, they could
eliminate their dependence on imported grain.

The next priority for LDCs is to control population growth so
that economic growth translates to improved per capita living
standards. If the number of children per family remains the same

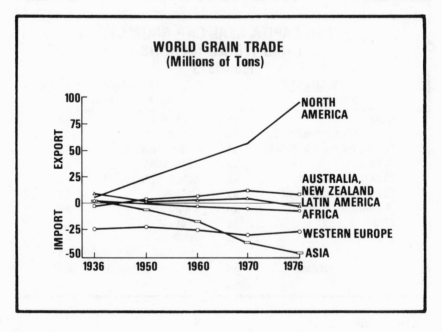

Figure 4.24

worldwide, total population will double by the year 2010 (Figure 4.25). Most of the population increase will come in developing countries. On the other hand, if an average of two children per family were achieved by 1990, the total projected world population increase would be reduced by almost one-half by 2010.

Developed nations should continue to provide aid to LDCs to help solve their most pressing problems. Equally important, developed nations must keep their markets open to LDC products. Non-oil LDCs have had a trade deficit with the U.S. every year except one since 1960 (Figure 4.26). LDC exports also have been increasingly affected by the imposition of import quotas and other restraints by the U.S. and other developed nations.

The fact that the industrialized nations have erected barriers to trade in such areas as shoes, textiles, and sugar not only has hurt particular LDC exports, but has signalled that the developed nations do not welcome too much competition from LDCs. This

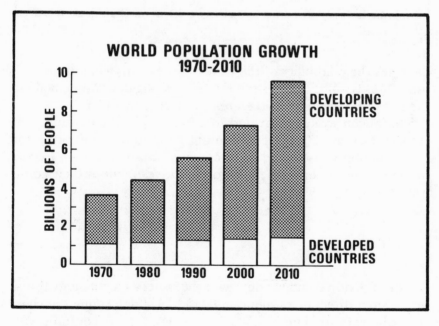

Figure 4.25

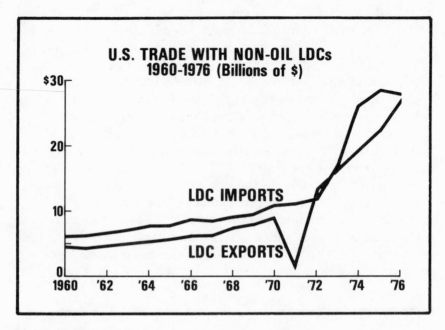

Figure 4.26

damages the credibility of the developed nations' commitment to the LDCs, as well as the desirability of pursuing development along the lines of Taiwan and other relatively successful LDCs.

Special concessions provided to LDCs under the existing generalized system of preferences might be used as a substitute for LDC commitments to reduce their own import controls, export subsidies, and other barriers to foreign investment in their countries.

CONCLUSIONS

How individual nations deal with the issues of technology transfer, foreign direct investment, and trade will determine the character of our future international economic order. To continue with the relative openness we now enjoy, individual nations will have to adopt policies that get their own domestic economic houses in order. This will require politically difficult adjustments by government, industry, and labor in each nation. It will require strategic planning to anticipate problems and deal with them before they become major. Finally, it will require a better understanding of the importance of private enterprise in general, and of the multinational corporation in particular, to help solve the most pressing economic problems.

Developed nations must adopt policies aimed at stimulating noninflationary domestic economic expansion. Control of inflation must become the top economic priority of each nation. To date, most countries have gone about this in precisely the wrong way. They have drawn their ideas about controlling the money supply from the monetarist school, and have drawn ideas about consumer-oriented tax reductions from the imitators of Keynes. Consequently, they have worked at cross purposes. Many governments have pursued expansion by raising consumer demand first, assuming this would set private investment in motion. Wage increases have exceeded the rate of inflation. Tax reductions have favored small and medium incomes. As a result of these widespread policies, national economies have displayed a common disease: a pronounced and chronic weakness in private capital spending.

Tax changes are needed to stimulate capital investment and technology development to improve the productivity of industries, create job opportunities and provide a solid foundation for noninflationary economic growth.

If such measures are not adopted, we likely will withdraw further into a protectionist mode, with the consequent reductions in economic growth, increases in inflation, and loss of living standard. Perhaps more fundamentally, it would threaten our political institutions and raise serious questions about the continued commitment to democracy.

Developing nations must place more emphasis on what they can do to help themselves. They must focus on solving their most immediate problems of food and population, and on developing the intellectual infrastructure capable of absorbing technologies that are transferred from the developed countries.

Most of the bilateral problems must be dealt with in a multilateral context. New international mechanisms for cooperation need to be explored. One possibility for the U.S., Canada, and Mexico would be formation of a North American Economic Union. This Union could work on a wide range of labor, energy, and economic problems and coordinate programs of mutual benefit.

International organizations such as the U.N. must replace rhetoric with constructive proposals that take into account the interests and needs of all parties. This includes a greater appreciation by LDC governments of the benefits multinational corporations can provide to LDCs pursuing their modernization strategies. Hopefully, what is presumed to be an inherent conflict can be translated into opportunities that benefit all parties.

The time for decisive action is now. If the current trends are not reversed, the very survival of our political and economic institutions could be threatened.

NOTES

1. U.S. Department of Commerce figures.
2. Figure given by George Perry of Brookings Institution, as quoted in *Business Week*, 20 December 1976; oil import numbers are from International Monetary Fund, *International Financial Statistics,* and from the Department of Energy.
3. Edward Denison, *Accounting for U.S. Economic Growth, 1929–69* (Washington, D.C.: Brookings Institution, 1972); Solomon Fabricant, "Perspective on the Capital Requirements Question," in *Capital for Productivity and Jobs* by the American Assembly, Columbia University (Englewood Cliffs, N.J.: Prentice-Hall, 1977).
4. The study was conducted by Martin S. Feldstein and Anthony Pellechio of Harvard University, cited in *Business Week,* 6 February 1978, p. 13.
5. U.S. Department of Commerce, *Selected Data on U.S. Direct Investment Abroad, 1966–76,* 1977.

6. Ibid.

7. United Nations, *Multinational Corporations in World Development,* (New York: Praeger, 1974); *O.E.C.D. Review,* 1977; International Monetary Fund, *International Monetary Studies.* The fifteen are Korea, Taiwan, Indonesia, Singapore, Colombia, Spain, Brazil, Philippines, El Salvador, Malaysia, Mexico, India, Kenya, Peru, and Argentina.

FIVE

The Private Sector in the Developing Countries

Moeen A. Qureshi

Executive Vice President
International Finance Corporation

In the postwar period the problems of economic development have figured prominently in economic and political discussions. Yet in the bulk of the development literature there is a notable absence of inquiry into the role of the private sector. This is also true of the official and unofficial documents which record the ongoing North-South debate. Aside from questions concerning multinational enterprises and foreign investment, these documents give the private sector scant attention.

I suspect many in this field, professionals and nonprofessionals alike, tend to equate the private sector with the market oriented developed countries and fail to recognize, except perhaps in the vaguest sort of way, the presence of the private sector in the Third

World. Others feel it is an intractable political problem and not susceptible to economic analysis. Still others feel that the proper role of the private sector is a question of national preference and thus not a legitimate subject for global inquiries on development problems.

Yet, given these legitimate concerns, the fact remains that three-quarters of the Gross Domestic Product of the Third World is generated by the private sector. In spite of this, little is known about what the private sector can and cannot do; little is known about how to direct the energies of the private sector towards a general improvement in the welfare of the people. In other words there is a serious lack of understanding of the elements making up the role of the private sector in development.

The purpose of this chapter is not to put one or more of these elements under a microscope. Instead, I would like to discuss a few considerations that I feel are basic to the setting within which these elements could be discussed. These thoughts are directed, then, to those who are just starting out on an inquiry into the role of the private sector.

Although the role of the private sector in development has not been well explored and the dynamics of it are too little understood, there are some things we do know. The issues relating to the relationships between the private and public sectors are not confined just to the developing countries. However, the debate over the role of the private sector in developing countries tends to be more controversial and divisive. This is because (a) the private sector in these countries shows all the attributes and deficiencies of underdevelopment; (b) the debate over private versus public often takes on a strong ideological flavor and therefore biases and inhibits open debate; and (c) the controversy regarding the multinational corporations and foreign investment, by looming so large, tends to cloud our understanding of the underlying issues.

It has often been my experience that when the issue of the role of the private sector is raised, the result is to raise ideological spectors. Arguments tend to polarize, people start lining up behind moral embattlements, and absolute concepts are flung back and forth with righteous indignation. Meanwhile, the issue remains un-explored in no-man's-land even though both sides have retired with their ideologies largely intact. Over cocktails this can, at worst, be amusing; over an international conference table, the effects can be explosive.

As the matter of the private sector in development is pursued, it is necessary to keep in mind that ideologies are useful, even neces-sary, in that they provide us with norms from which to view the world. They are inspirational, but they are rarely authoritative guides. Therefore it is not necessary, and is perhaps dangerous, to consider the private sector as a concept having value in and of itself.

Closely associated with the problem of ideologies is the problem of polar terms and definitions. We all know that Newtonian physics rested on mental pictures that reduced all phenomena to energy and matter. Matter was little lumps of which the atom was the smallest. Time was a sequence and space was a frame. Over the years, scientists struggled, with decreasing success, to explain the world in terms of these images. Scientific discovery became mired in these images because they could not be used to describe a world in which time was a dimension and matter a form of energy. Unfortunately, many of the social sciences, especially political economy, give the appearance of being mired in somewhat the same problem.

To describe this situation, Thurmond Arnold introduced, many years ago in *The Folklore of Capitalism,* his notion of "polar terms." Polar terms are concepts which require an opposite in order for them to have meaning. For example, "private sector" has little meaning apart from the concept of "public sector." Therein lies the problem. Inquiries into the role of the private sector are often ideological debates with attendant moral attachments presenting a choice between two polar concepts: that of traditional "free enter-prise" on the one hand and a "social responsibility" creed on the other. Both concepts are loaded with moral judgments and their own sets of images or mental pictures that decreasingly reflect real world conditions.

A prime example of the confusion generated by the preconceived images embodied in the use of our polar concepts is the question, What is the private sector? If we limit our inquiry to productive undertakings, there traditionally have been two yardsticks for defining privateness: Who owns the assets, and who controls the decision making? Unfortunately, it turns out that neither is a very good absolute measure.

For most of us, ownership is the criterion most often evoked to provide us with an image of the private sector. We have been able partially to overcome the polar concepts trap by introducing classes within the extremes. Thus we have established images of government ownership, mixed government and private ownership with government majority, mixed with private majority, and wholly private. Ideologically, however, the images evoked to differentiate the private from the public sector are still at the extremes of the stereotype—wholly government or wholly private ownership.

Now consider the possibility of having decision making as the most important criterion. Given the realities of today's world, where social, political, and economic objectives have become indistinguishable, ownership carries with it less and less the rights of decision making and of freedom of action; there is not even a guarantee of responsiveness to market forces. Although it may be perfectly legitimate to lean more towards decision making as the criterion of public or private ownership, this criterion is even less subject to quantification and thus less likely to provoke solid images. Consider the following example:

A manufacturing enterprise is owned 100 percent by a financial institution, 51 percent of whose equity is owned by government. The financial institution relies on the private capital market for the sale of its securities, and its own investments are expected to yield a rate of return sufficiently high to maintain its position in the capital market. Consequently, its directive to the manufacturing enterprise is to maximize its profits. Within these limits the enterprise has substantial autonomy. Is this a public or private enterprise?

The truth of the matter is that there is no single "correct" definition of the private sector, nor should we attempt to define it with such precision. The definition must rest on some elements of private ownership and private decision making, but there are no fixed ratios or mixes.

There is another problem in exploring the role of the private sector in developing countries. The very statement of the issue gives the impression that there is in fact THE role of the private sector in development—implying that one can precisely define what the role is in all countries and in all circumstances. Actually nothing is further from the truth. This role has not been well defined even in the developed countries, much less in the developing countries.

In years past this was less of a problem. In the United States, as in most other industrialized nations, laissez-faire was accepted as the creed of the nation. But all the industrialized nations, the United States included, have now dropped even any pretense of pointing to the absolutes of laissez-faire as practical solutions to social, political, and even economic problems. Emmette Redford summed up the situation well in saying, "What characterizes American governmental interventions in the economy is empirical response to particular situations, problems and pressing human needs."[1] This situation is not vastly different in the developing countries. The outcomes, the means, and the degree of intervention into economic affairs may be different, but it must be understood that they are responding to a different set of situations, problems, and human needs.

At this point it is possible to start putting the pieces of this inquiry back together. The best place to start is with the question, What is the current thinking on economic development and what is its challenge?

In the past five years or so, development thinking has undergone a great upheaval. One of the first casualties has been the so-called "trickle down" theory of economic development. It reputedly lies in shambles—excommunicated by the development community. The current thought is that a general rise of GNP in the developing countries does not necessarily mean a general rise in the well-being of a majority of the people. The development community pays much more heed today to the distribution of the fruits of development. While growth is essential given the low income per capita in most of the developing world, there is justifiable concern to ensure that the development process will bring about a genuine betterment in the condition of the mass of the people, that it will serve to meet basic human needs, and that one of its major objectives will be to help eradicate absolute poverty. This shifting emphasis from growth, as such, to a broader range of societal problems has come about partially in response to a better understanding of the enormity of the development challenge and a better recognition of the time bomb that is ticking away within the poorest segments of humanity.

The task is this: About 800 million people in the developing world have income levels below that needed to meet basic food requirements. The scale of absolute poverty is even larger if we expand our notion of minimum levels of living to include access to essential public services such as education, health services, clean water, sanitation, and shelter. Over one billion people—more than one-half the population in the developing world—do not have access to these essential services.

Furthermore, it is estimated that 80 percent of the poor live in rural areas, concentrated mainly in the poorest countries in South Asia and sub-Saharan Africa. This implies that a large part of the strategy for poverty alleviation must be directed to raising incomes in rural areas, since the capacity for absorbing the population in the nonagricultural sector is limited even with that sector's rapid expansion.

Another way of seeing the challenge is to measure it against what it would take to raise the developing world to the standard enjoyed here in the United States. The algebra of closing the absolute gap in per capita incomes can be summarized as follows: If the developing countries manage to double their per capita growth rate while the U.S. maintains its historical growth, among the fastest growing developing countries only a handful—at most six to seven—would be able to close the gap within 100 years, and only another nine within 1,000 years.

What can be done? First of all, it is quite obvious that the income gaps between the developed and developing world cannot be closed within either our lifetime or the lifetimes of many generations to come; it is unrealistic to think in those terms. What about the elimination of poverty? This proposition when looked at realistically does not appear within our immediate grasp either. If not that, what about abolishing absolute poverty by the end of this century? World Bank studies suggest that even this does not appear feasible given the political constraints under which governments operate. Then, what *is* feasible?

A realistic assessment of the scope for improving the lot of the poorest will have to be set at achieving significant progress towards poverty alleviation by the year 2000. What does this mean?

With some optimistic combination of policy and outcomes, it may be possible to reduce the incidence of absolute poverty from about one-half of the population in the low-income developing countries to about one-quarter of their population by the year 2000. But even achieving this will require a massive mobilization of resources. It will require about a doubling of the growth rates in those countries and considerably more concessionary assistance from the developed world. It will require agricultural growth rates of about 4 percent per annum, a shift to much more labor intensive patterns of growth in the nonagricultural sectors, and a redirection of public expenditures into those areas that directly affect the welfare and incomes of the poorest.

Of course, reducing the levels of absolute poverty, or even increasing assistance to the poorest countries, is not the entire challenge before the development community. The middle-income countries' goal of achieving more than a minimum standard of living for their peoples cannot be allowed to go unfulfilled.[2] It is in these countries that the seeds of rising expectations have been most firmly implanted, and it is also here that we find the greatest indigenous capability to accelerate the development process and attain a measure of economic self-reliance. What this group of countries needs is the opportunity to participate in the international division of labor, and access to both developed country markets and the international financial market place. To achieve this will require more sympathetic understanding by the developed world of the problems these middle-income countries face, especially of the priority which industrialization has in their further economic and social progress. But most of all it will require forging a new understanding of the role and responsibilities of private enterprise, both indigenous and foreign, so that their latent potential for development can be fully exploited.

The task is enormous, but given the parameters it is both feasible and necessary to fulfill the goal at least in part. It is not an impossible task. However, whether in terms of the transfer of resources or of the effort the developing countries must make themselves to meet their basic needs, the task of development is so vast that it calls for the fullest possible deployment of all available resources.

A fact about development that is often overlooked is that the private sector generates almost three-quarters of the Gross Domestic Product of developing countries. The bulk of this is within the rural agricultural sector—the very target area for reducing absolute poverty. Just on the basis of its sheer weight the argument for the need to mobilize the private sector would be sufficient. Any developing country which either ignores or overlooks the potential of the private sector is most surely robbing itself of the possibility of meeting even the modest development goals set out earlier.

But there is a more basic reason why the private sector must be mobilized: In order for the developing countries to generate a sustainable and lasting climb out of poverty, the motivation and energy for the effort must come from the grass roots, whether in rural or urban areas. In order to harness the individual and collective talents of the people, there must be a way for people to help themselves. It is only through programs of self-help that the poorest groups in our societies find the means to increase their productivity and to find earning opportunities. This effort must, of course, go in tandem with the efforts of the public sector to provide the setting, the infrastructure, within which self-help efforts can be successful. Likewise, concessionary assistance can provide the springboard for the initial push. But the motivation is bound to

falter unless people have the opportunity to quickly learn to swim
on their own once they hit the water.

We all know that, in the developing world, local government and
private enterprise have often been at odds. Governments have felt
that the private sector followed investment policies which distorted
national economic development objectives, and they have won-
dered whether the foreign private investment contribution compensated for its economic and social costs. For its part, the private
sector has felt that government policies distorted the market and
obstructed the achievement of profitability for private investors.
Foreign investors, in particular, have seen government attitudes as
irrational or discriminatory, or both, and have felt they were not
sufficiently compensated for the risks and uncertainties they faced.
The result has been, at worst, direct confrontation between government and the private sector and, even at best, strained relationships rooted in a continuing crisis of confidence.

The effect of this situation has been to reduce the contribution
that the private sector is capable of making to the development of
the Third World. It stands to reason that that contribution cannot
be made fully in an atmostphere of latent if not open hostility
between government and the private sector. Yet the participation,
the mobilization, of the private sector in development is not, to the
developing world, a choice. If this is not done, even the very modest
development objectives will not be accomplished. Thus the fric-
tions between the private and public sectors must be resolved.

There have been various attempts to defuse this kind of situation
and such developments are welcome. But to my mind they do not
go very far towards creating a new relationship between governments and private sectors. As a first step in that direction, I suggest
the need for a more universal recognition of the problem and a
more global search for solutions.

As governments debate the issues of economic development
there needs to be a more explicit recognition of the role of the
private sector. In documents issued regarding a New Economic
Order, only scant attention has been paid to the role of the private

sector, outside of references to foreign investment and the multinational enterprises. The response of the developed countries has been just as meager.

I sometimes think that in the international economic debate the private sector is viewed like the crazy uncle whom the family keeps up in the attic—everyone hears him trashing about up there, but it is considered impolite to talk about him. What everyone seems to forget is that we are not dealing here with an ancient and senile creature but with a very live-and-kicking member of the family who just might prove to be the leader of the development process. There is a need at this level to recognize the problem, to deal with it explicitly, and to ensure that the private sector is fitted into any scheme of solutions regarding the development of the world's economies.

To sum up, the recognition of the need to improve relationships between the private and public sectors does not rest upon ideological grounds, nor does it require a choice between polar concepts such as state versus private ownership. It does require the understanding that a large part of the wealth created in the world, and particularly in the developing world, is created through the private sector. Furthermore, it requires the recognition that this situation is not going to change in the very near future. Above all, it requires an acceptance of the fact that it is about time the current attitudes of confrontation between the public and private sectors be replaced by a "compact" which will enable the developing nations to achieve at least those modest development goals for which they clearly have the potential.

As each nation has its own problems, its own social, economic, and political pressures, it must evolve its own particular "compact." Nevertheless, we are not looking at a problem that is confined to any one country, nor, for that matter, is it confined just to the developing countries. The heart of the problem is the need to harness the individual and collective talents of all people. This is a global concern and, therefore, in a sense, we are talking about a global compact.

What are some of the more universal elements that would form part of such a compact?

Let me take first the challenge facing the typical private enterprise, domestic or foreign, in a developing country. Many more calculations than just the interests of shareholders now need to be taken into account. Such an enterprise needs to be sensitive to the economic and social priorities of the government and to its natural anxiety that the benefits of any private enterprise should contribute effectively to national progress. The elements of this side of the equation are not usually, if ever, spelled out with any degree of clarity.

For its part, the local government needs to be sensitive to the need to create a setting in which private enterprise can best make its contribution. This is to say, it should recognize that against a background of general political and economic stability—and to the extent that the government can assure such stability—much will depend on the fiscal, monetary, and foreign exchange policies it pursues. More than that, a government should adopt and adhere to a clearly stated set of economic ground rules to provide a coherent and assured setting within which private enterprise can contribute to the general welfare.

The private sector in the developing countries, fueled either by domestic or foreign investment, or both, can contribute effectively to the economic and social progress of the country only if it can work in a conducive environment. That environment is created when government sees private enterprise as responsive to the needs of society and private enterprise sees government as willing to provide the framework within which that response can most effectively be made. In short, the existence of a community of interest, even a sense of partnership, between them should be recognized by government and the general public, on the one side, and by the private sector, on the other. This is the essence of the "compact" idea.

Many will think that the kind of world economic relationships I have discussed, and, within them, the kinds of relationships between the public and private sectors in the developing countries, are quite unattainable. I am not so pessimistic. I come from a developing country and can lay claim to some understanding of their aspirations as well as their peculiarities and problems. More important, I now find myself in an institution, the International Finance Corporation, which is dedicated precisely to the task of promoting this partnership between the public and private sectors at both a national and a global level. IFC's experience over the last twenty years or so, during which it has worked with both developing and industrialized countries, confirms that these new relationships can be created—if only because it is in the common interest that they should be.

NOTES

1. Emmette Redford, *American Government and the Economy* (New York: Macmillan Co., 1965), p. 632.
2. Middle-income countries are those with an average annual per capita income in the range of $500 to $1500.

SIX

The Role of Private Capital

in the World Economy

Paul A. Volcker

President
Federal Reserve Bank of New York

The role of private capital in the world economy is a large subject. It forces the economist and the practitioner to come to terms with some thorny conceptual problems and real-world paradoxes. Any generalization is subject to qualification. No two countries have the same political and economic circumstances—and their perceptions sometimes differ more than their objective circumstances. Our only recourse is to impose some reasonable boundaries on the discussion from the start. To that end, I want to focus on three groups of issues.

First, there is the question of the extent to which we can be guided by underlying economic principles. There is a body of theory to justify the notion that unfettered private capital movements from one country to another would enhance economic development and wealth. But if that theory tells us international shifts of funds are mutually beneficial, why do so many countries maintain batteries of restrictions to control them?

Second, we can readily observe the increasing role of private capital markets and institutions as intermediaries between ultimate borrower and lender. More specifically, massive amounts of funds have been "recycled" through the major international, and most particularly U.S.-based, banks. International bond markets have also expanded to a degree that few would have imagined possible ten years ago.

We can explore the degree to which the theoretical benefits of free private capital movements hold up in a situation where the great bulk of the flows reflect extensions of debt, often of a short-term character, responsive to current interest rate differentials and to governmental decision, rather than the kind of longer term profit opportunities motivating direct investment. Because the distinction between private and official flows often becomes blurred when a government is the ultimate borrower, or sometimes the lender, we need to ask ourselves whether this hybrid activity should or could be governed by some general principles.

Third, we are led to questions of broad public policy. There is a good deal of controversy among those who feel that the role of private capital has been too large and those who feel it can and should be larger. Those in the first group usually seek to expand the relative contribution of official financing. The others are more concerned with reducing and eliminating existing impediments to private capital flows.

These are the kinds of issues that are easier to raise than to resolve, at least in a way that will command a high degree of unanimity. That is because they are real issues and contentious issues. They confront economists and practitioners alike with viewpoints differing with circumstances. But without promising all the answers, we can at least try to improve our understanding of the questions. That, after all, provides a start toward reaching some consensus on a framework for guiding public policies and attitudes.

THE POTENTIAL BENEFITS AND COSTS
OF PRIVATE CAPITAL MOVEMENTS

Let me start with the simplest theory. Consider two countries. In the first, there are projects available that are expected to yield 20 per cent per annum. In the second, the best projects available are expected to yield only 5 per cent per annum.

In those circumstances, we can readily show both countries are likely to be better off if investors in the second country can put some of their money into the higher yielding projects in the first. The investors can earn a higher rate of return on their capital. The receiving country can increase output at a greater rate of speed while maintaining consumption. In concept, total world output and income is increased enough to compensate any individuals who, in the process, might have suffered a decline in income—for example, workers in either country who might be displaced from existing employment by the new project, or who might have been employed in an alternative low-yielding project in the capital exporting country.

Certainly, there are a variety of secondary effects that would influence the exact outcome. For one thing, a sequence of trade surpluses and deficits for the two countries could be set off, disturbing existing employment patterns. Those effects are difficult or impossible to trace in detail. But under a wide range of reasonable assumptions, the conclusion that there are mutual benefits should hold up.

At this level of abstraction, the parallel with elementary trade theory is evident. When resources and production patterns differ among countries, trade among them should produce benefits for each. The gain results because each country tends to specialize in producing those goods for which it is comparatively efficient. Or put another way, each produces more of the goods for which it can potentially earn a relatively higher rate of return.

In practice, we know that every country has thought of reasons of one kind or another to influence trade through tariffs, quantitative restrictions, or otherwise. One classic argument is to protect an infant industry until it grows large enough to enjoy economies of scale that enable it to stand on its own. Another argument is to protect workers in a declining industry subject to foreign competition. Occasionally, a country can take advantage of market position and use restrictions on imports or exports (as in the case of OPEC) to improve its total welfare at the expense of others. But despite all these deviations in practice from the theoretical ideal, the fact that the general doctrine of the mutual benefits of liberal trade is recognized and well entrenched is far from meaningless. It has provided a sense of known direction—a standard—by which to judge progress and measure deviations. There is, in fact, a kind of built in pressure to resist temptation to "beggar thy neighbor," in the familiar phrase, or, more positively, to maintain an harmonious trading environment. The doctrine has, in fact, spawned an international organization—GATT—to serve as a watchdog against abusive trade restrictions. It has led to repeated multilateral negotiations in the postwar period to reduce trade barriers. It has helped provide the political will and understanding to maintain a relatively open trading world in the wake of the strains of the oil crisis and recession.

The commitment to the principle of free movement of private capital has been substantially weaker. It is not really hard to understand why. The gains from investment, extended out over a long period of time, may seem more abstract. Uncertainty and the possibility of expectations deviating from later reality are present in all investment decisions, so the textbook assumptions may more plausibly be challenged in "real life" circumstances. We have plenty of experience showing capital flows responding to volatile anticipations of political developments, policy measures, or exchange rate changes—events that may or may not turn out to be linked to fundamental economic trends and incentives. Moreover, countries do not have the luxury of ignoring the effects of capital flows on the distribution of employment and incomes, just because theory says that, in principle, gains will exceed losses.

Perhaps most important, governmental authorities may have a different planning horizon than that of private investors, and different priorities than those of the market. In many instances, balance of payments and exchange rate considerations have seemed decisive in the short run. It is one thing to assert that profitable investments abroad—either direct investments or port-folio investments in financial assets—will eventually strengthen the balance of payments of the capital exporting country. It is another thing to be so forward-looking at a time when the immediate payments position is weak, the currency is depreciating, or both. When exchange rates were fixed, the temptation to resort to capital controls to protect the rate was particularly strong, for little im-mediate cost seemed to be attached to such controls relative to the political and economic problems of an exchange rate change. Con-sequently, a good many countries have tried to insulate the cur-rency from the effects of capital outflows by exchange restrictions.

In a world of floating exchange rates, the pressures have not disappeared, because the exchange rate has a pivotal role in in-fluencing domestic prices, costs, and output. Some countries, espe-cially the U.S., have acted to dismantle many or all of their previous controls, and I believe it is clear that open markets for the U.S. have a key role to play in the effective functioning of the world economy. But elsewhere many controls remain. We have also seen some recent examples of governments resorting to new controls—especially on the inward flow of capital—in an effort to achieve their exchange rate objectives.

In these latter cases, there has been a fear of the effects of an appreciating currency on domestic output and employment. Moreover, increased foreign deposits in the banking system may complicate the task of monetary control. Compounding the prob-lem from the standpoint of theory, domestic interest rates in an appreciating currency country are often below those abroad, so that capital seems to be flowing uphill. (Of course, what counts for theory is real and not nominal interest rates, and real interest rates cannot be directly observed.) In these instances, the apparent yield disadvantage does not outweigh the expectation of short-term gains from an exchange rate appreciation.

One response to these kinds of events has been to limit the types of short-term domestic financial assets nonresidents may acquire.

But bonds, equities, or real estate can be purchased as speculative vehicles by those who are kept from other investment outlets. So a country inclined toward controls may find itself driven into restrictions and more and more restrictions; perhaps the more meaningful message is the difficulty of setting up and implementing controls when markets are so well developed that they can quickly find new ways around any new controls.

The responses of some countries, particularly in the developing world, to direct investment inflows represent a quite different kind of departure from the principle of free capital flows. Those are the countries that may well have my hypothetical 20 percent per annum projects available to be tapped, reflecting a scarcity of capital and an abundance of unemployed and underemployed workers. Moreover, they may be especially short of those technological, managerial, and marketing skills that multinational companies bring with them when they invest in a country. Nevertheless, those countries frequently appear willing to erect barriers against foreign direct investment that, on the face of it, would seem to bring clear economic benefits.

The reason is bound up, of course, in the complex (and sometimes conflicting) social, political, and economic objectives that underlie a development effort. Local ownership and control is given a special priority. Governments are sensitive to the speed with which foreign influences can be absorbed in a traditional society. The opposition can be rooted in ideology.

But governments in developing countries may also rationalize controls on direct investment on narrower economic terms. For example, authorities may themselves attach low priority to high-yield investment projects; in economic jargon, they view the social returns as different from the private returns. And that judgment may not be based entirely on social priorities, but on the hard-headed recognition that other distortions in the economy—import quotas for example—may be reflected in sheltered markets that artificially push up the private rate of return.

More generally, there are suspicions that foreign firms may not tailor production methods to the kinds of resources available in the host country, and that their commitment may not be lasting. Multinational companies are criticized for choosing a set of blueprints more appropriate to their capital-rich home base and applying it indiscriminately in the labor-abundant LDCs.

One can wonder about the validity of these particular complaints; there is ample evidence that many poorer countries are intrigued by the latest technology in projects undertaken by themselves, and may be drawn into government financing of projects that seem fashionable but are of a scale or type out of keeping with their resources and natural markets.

But there can be no doubt that controls on direct investments are a fact of life in many countries, however strongly the presumption in favor of free flows of capital is pressed. Typically, investments in certain industries may be reserved entirely for local residents. In other instances, joint ownership may be required, perhaps with local control. Business operations may be restricted; for example, a certain proportion of output may have to be exported. Foreign enterprises may not be allowed to raise funds internally. There are usually regulations governing repatriation of profits.

Given the obstacles—not to mention the occasional expropriations of foreign investments that have occurred—the fact is direct investment by the U.S. has increased far beyond expectations two decades ago, and has spread far beyond the traditional area of resource development (Table 6.1). Twenty years ago, Europe was the prime area for investment, predominantly from the U.S. To-

**Table 6.1 United States Direct Investment Flows
(Annual Averages, Billions of Dollars)**

	1960–1964	1965–1969	1970–1973	1974–1976
Industrial countries	2.3	3.7	6.4	8.8
Oil-exporting countries[1]	0.0	0.1	−0.4	−1.3
All other countries	0.8	1.2	2.0	4.1
Total	3.1	4.0	8.0	11.6

Source: Department of Commerce
[1] Middle East and Venezuela

day, the investment is much more broadly spread, both among those making and among those receiving the investment. Notably, developing countries have attracted an increasing share. The total flow of direct investments from the industrial countries to the developing countries grew from less than $2 billion a year in the early sixties to over $3.5 billion by the early seventies and then to $8 billion in 1976 (Table 6.2).

Table 6.2   Direct Investment Flows from Industrial Countries to Developing Countries (Billions of Dollars)

Year	Amount
1961	1.8
1962	1.5
1963	1.6
1964	1.6
1965	2.5
1966	2.2
1967	2.1
1968	3.2
1969	2.9
1970	3.5
1971	3.6
1972	4.5
1973	6.7
1974	7.1
1975	10.3
1976	8.0

Sources: World Bank *Annual Report,* 1977; O.E.C.D., *Flow of Resources to Developing Countries,* Paris, 1973.

In the broadest terms, this development seems to accord with theory. As postwar reconstruction in Europe was completed and the benefits of the Common Market absorbed, highly profitable opportunities in that area became scarcer. At the same time, developing countries offered the potential for high rates of return on invested capital, particularly as open markets for manufactured goods enabled them to take advantage of their cheap labor. Foreign investment helped to support faster rates of growth and enabled countries to build modern infrastructures. Those developments in turn helped attract more investment. This self-reinforcing process did not by itself cure every economic problem that a developing country faced. But it did provide a positive stimulus in a large number of countries. Generally speaking, those countries most receptive to foreign investment in general, and to direct investment in particular, not only attracted the multinational companies, but experienced the fastest sustained growth.

All of this suggests to me the force of the simple textbook presumption that the flow of private direct investment can indeed make a strong contribution to economic welfare. The barriers raised to that flow are often explicable, at least on the surface, in terms of other objectives. But one is left with a question as to whether many governments, in tipping the scales for or against new barriers (or in removing the old), weigh heavily enough the benefits of investment that can only be realized over time. One is left with the further question as to whether new techniques and methods might be developed by individual countries or multilaterally that would induce more investment in an acceptable political and economic framework. That is a question to which I will return shortly.

But first, I want to comment on the private international capital markets—bank lending, bond financing, and other forms of capital that do not entail management control. After all, direct investment represented much less than half of the total private funds that flowed from the industrial to the developing countries in recent years. The contrast is even more striking for those industrial countries that have been net recipients of private flows. Together, they had net private capital inflows through international money and capital markets of about $17½ billion in 1976, for instance, as against actual net outflows of direct investment of $5 billion.

THE ROLE OF PRIVATE CAPITAL MARKETS

The benefits and potential problems of private capital markets can be illustrated by the experience since the 1973 oil crisis. Obviously, in important ways, that experience has been unique—unique in the scale of international lending activity generally, and more particularly in the size of the net flows of funds from surplus to deficit countries. Partly because of the exceptional scale, some of the underlying issues have been thrown into sharper focus.

The world was indeed fortunate at the time of the oil price shock of 1973–74 to have in place an apparatus for handling the unprecedented shift that occurred in international payments positions and in national wealth. That apparatus included not just the national banking systems and capital markets of the U.S., and to a lesser extent of other developed countries. It also included, most importantly, the Eurocurrency market—a short-term deposit and loan market—nurtured by the large international banks, and the Eurobond market supported by banks, investment houses, and other financial institutions. These mechanisms for making private capital available were supplemented by existing and expanded credit facilities of international organizations, particularly the International Monetary Fund and the World Bank. But the private markets had to carry most of the action (Table 6.3).

This apparatus developed strongly long before the oil crisis despite—indeed partly because of—rather widespread use of controls on international capital flows during the period of fixed exchange rates. In the Bretton Woods system, such controls, if not actually officially encouraged, were viewed relatively benignly, certainly relative to controls on current transactions. But markets found a way to operate around the controls, partly by encouraging the growth of so-called "off shore" markets outside national control mechanisms. The very considerable size international capital markets had achieved by 1973—from a standing start after World War II—is itself testimony to the strong economic incentives to borrow and lend across national boundaries.

At any rate, when the world moved to a system of greater exchange rate flexibility, many of the existing controls were relaxed

Table 6.3 International Financial Credit Flows, 1974–77 (Annual Averages, Billions of Dollars)

	Private credit			Official credit		Total
	Bank credit					
	From 8 European countries[1]	From U.S.[4]	New bond issues[5]	Use of IMF credit[6]	Multilateral & bilateral credits[7]	
Industrial countries	26.8[2]	4.6	16.3	2.3	3.8	53.8
Oil-exporting countries	3.3[3]	0.8	0.3	0.0	0.4	4.8
All other countries	22.8	11.0	1.9	2.1	11.8	49.6
Total	52.9	16.5	18.5	4.4	16.0	108.2

[1]Belgium-Luxembourg, France, Germany, Italy, Netherlands, Sweden, Switzerland, and United Kingdom. Annual averages for December 1974–September 1977, includes interbank placements. Source: BIS.
[2]Excludes Austria, Denmark, and Norway.
[3]Middle East.
[4]Includes interbank placements. Source: U.S. *Treasury Bulletin*.
[5]Source: Morgan Guaranty, *World Financial Markets*.
[6]Source: IMF, *International Financial Statistics*.
[7]Source: OECD, *Development Cooperation*, 1977, and Federal Reserve Bank of New York staff estimates. Annual averages are for 1974–1976 for oil-exporting and all other countries. Credits to industrial countries include EC lending to member countries and estimates of bilateral lending (including OPEC lending).
Note: Figures may not add to totals due to rounding.

117

or eliminated and the opportunity for integration of domestic and international financial markets increased enormously. The dramatic rise in oil prices, occurring at about the same time as the dismantling of capital controls in the U.S., soon produced forces that sharply increased demands on those markets.

The direct effect of the quadrupling of oil prices was an enormous OPEC surplus, peaking at close to $70 billion in 1974 and falling to about $35 billion in 1977. Those surpluses were matched by an equal collective deficit on the part of the oil consuming countries. But the recent imbalances have been even larger than these aggregates imply, because the deficits have not been spread at all evenly among consuming countries. Some industrial countries still have a current surplus, while others, including the U.S., have large deficits.

In any event, the result was a small group of necessitous lenders—the OPEC countries that could not invest at home all the funds generated by their current account surpluses—and a larger group of necessitous borrowers, who had to cover current account deficits.

For the most part, the lenders and borrowers did not link up directly; they went through intermediaries. Petroleum producers, being initially conservative in their lending practices and seeking high returns on short-term investments, placed large amounts of deposits in the Eurocurrency market. Deficit nations, actively seeking balance of payments financing, went to the same market to borrow. This process of moving funds from OPEC savers to borrowers around the world, especially through the Eurobanking system, goes by the rather unedifying name of "recycling." In fact, it is simply "cycling," or more precisely, the traditional intermediation function of banks—borrowing short-term funds and lending for the somewhat longer term—applied on an international scale.

Conceptually, following the lines of my earlier analysis, bank (or other) intermediaries provide the service of moving loan funds from relatively low-yield areas to those with high yields. Broadly, I think the concept is reflected in the practice: The yield on marginal investments in the domestic economies of oil countries, particularly the high surplus Persian Gulf states, can in the short run be thought of as practically zero, because physical and human constraints to the expansion of investment are much more binding than those countries' supply of financial capital.

But as we look more closely, we can also see some practical questions regarding the extent to which we can rely on market incentives alone to direct capital to points of need. In the wake of the oil crisis, a considerable amount of international capital went to countries as general balance of payments financing, unrelated to specific projects or investment activity. Indeed, such lending can appropriately be provided to deficit economies on an ongoing basis only if the fundamental assumptions of the simple theory are respected—that is, if the funds are eventually used, directly or indirectly, for productive investment that earns sufficient returns to service the debt. But that link is not assured in balance of payments financing; the decision to borrow is typically made by government and backed in the first instance by its promise to pay, not by investment projects attractive on their own merits.

Under immediate balance of payments pressure, governments had a strong incentive to find new sources of funds abroad, and banks willingly took on the role of providing short- and medium-term balance of payments financing on the general credit of the country. This money certainly and understandably went, in part, to sustaining consumption levels, as oil-consuming countries acted to avoid a very rapid adjustment of living standards to the higher oil prices. Without that financing, the world could have faced a much more disruptive period, characterized by a more severe recession and a breakdown of liberal trade.

But there have been dangers in the process as well. The distinction between public and private borrowing was blurred when governments and public enterprises in deficit countries became the principal borrowers. They in turn channeled the funds to a variety of uses in the economy, often without the market disciplines assumed by theory.

Another factor helped stimulate the supply of funds. Domestic loan demand in the capital-rich, developed countries was particularly slack during, and in the aftermath of, recession. Intermediaries, looking to maximize returns, were perhaps more prone to lend to the rest of the world than their longer term relative rates of return implied. But clearly much of the international lending, although short-term in form, would have to be maintained for years to avoid abrupt adjustment difficulties.

As a result, we can identify some potential problems—for the lenders, for the borrowers, for those responsible for banking supervision—that are not explicitly treated in the simple theoretical view of capital movements. While some of the normal market disciplines were attenuated, the concept of sovereign, or country, risk assumed new importance. Country risk is a subtle and many-faceted concept. Oversimplifying, we can say it concerns all matters that affect the ability of a nation as a whole to service its external debt—to generate foreign exchange—in both the short and the long run. Evaluation of country risk entails certain different, and in some ways more complex, problems than traditional lending functions, which are geared primarily to the prospects for particular investments and particular company borrowers.

The country risk problem focuses attention more sharply on the mechanisms for so-called balance of payments adjustment, in other words, the means by which countries can restore their balance of payments positions and earn foreign exchange. Balance of payments adjustment, in turn, raises the most sensitive and difficult questions of both internal economic and exchange rate policies. The issues are typically as much political as economic. So we are left with a picture of private lenders closely concerned with the management of national governments. And in these circumstances, normal creditor/debtor relationships may not be fully applicable; disciplining or restraining a national government is not quite the same thing as dealing with a private company.

In a sense, there is an imbalance in the relationship. That imbalance can potentially be corrected by the participation of official lenders, particularly those international agencies specifically charged with the job of negotiating broad agreements with sovereign nations as part of their lending programs. The special responsibilities of the International Monetary Fund (IMF) for balance of payments financing are the prime case in point. A large part of the raison d'être of that institution is to meet the immediate balance of payments needs of its member institutions, but at the same time to insist upon economic policies that make the debt sustainable.

POLICY OPTIONS

No one can pretend to any certainty about what the best mix of private and official financing should be. Indeed, the extent of private international lending will remain large for the foreseeable future, and it has great advantages in terms of flexibility and the ability to marshall large amounts of funds without bureaucratic or political constraints. However, the role of official lenders, specifically the IMF, can be crucial, for at critical junctures it can step into situations that appear to involve risks beyond those appropriate to a private lender, and it can act to reduce those risks by insisting upon appropriate adjustment policies. Nevertheless, there is a real question today whether the IMF has enough resources to do that job effectively. The institution can hardly be persuasive in discussions of appropriate policies if its ability to provide funds to credit-worthy countries is severely limited.

I personally share the rather wide consensus among bankers, economists, and policymakers that official lending resources are not adequate today. In that connection, I can only welcome the initiatives underway to increase the funds available to the IMF. The action taken by the U.S. House of Representatives to support the so-called Witteveen Facility is an important step in that direction.

There are other areas where promising cooperation between official and private lenders can be facilitated. For instance, so-called co-financing or parallel financing, essentially bringing official and private institutions into the same lending syndicate, is sometimes a useful approach. At the very least, close exchanges of information will often be desirable, and the private lenders seem to me to have a self-interest in coordinating their actions with the policy objectives of the IMF.

For the longer run, it also seems appropriate to explore other innovative policy approaches to the problems surrounding international capital flows. As stated earlier, in the area of trade, the international community long ago evolved the General Agreement on Tariffs and Trade to lay down ground rules for equitable and consistent commercial policies, taking as their basic point of departure the mutual benefits of open and liberal trade. In an area where trade and capital directly overlap—the field of export credits— repeated efforts have been made, with at least limited success, to reach understandings on the terms and conditions of officially supported export credits; in fact, a new agreement negotiated among leading industrial countries took effect on April 1, 1978.[1]

We can potentially build on those precedents by extending this type of international understanding beyond the area of trade to the area of international investment. An approach toward some of those problems was made in 1976 when the OECD countries— encompassing most of the industrialized world—developed guidelines for the conduct of multinational enterprises and called for equitable treatment of international investment on terms consistent with the treatment of internal private investment.[2] A truly general arrangement, however, must include the developing economies as well. Such an agreement would help to facilitate the efficient movement of direct investment capital in accordance with the basic theory of resource allocation. It could potentially ease the problem of country risk that I alluded to earlier by clarifying the policies of debtor countries toward international investments.

I will not attempt here to specify the content of such a "General Agreement on International Investment." A great deal of discussion and negotiation would be required to meet varied interests. But I would contemplate that it might cover such matters as: nondiscriminatory national treatment of foreign investors where such investment is permitted; clearer understandings on appropriate compensation for nationalization of direct investment; procedures for the international review of investment controls or subsidies that are really designed to affect the flow of trade; general rules governing the use of controls for balance of payments purposes; and the responsibilities of multinational companies.

Obviously, a general agreement on international investment would be an ambitious undertaking—the work of years. But we have some base on which to build: The OECD rules for multinationals are a case in point. We also have important precedents in the field of trade and monetary affairs.

And perhaps most important, we have a strong incentive. Private international capital flows are enormous. The benefits are by now widely understood. But there is also growing awareness of some of the potential distortions and problems.

Borrowers and lenders have an immediate stake in maintaining an environment in which markets can continue to function and grow, but the implications extend far beyond their immediate interests. It is not too much to say that our prosperity, and that of the poorer countries, today more than ever before is bound up in the orderly international flow of private capital. To the degree that we can provide an agreed-upon and equitable framework for the conduct of that vital business, we can look forward with greater confidence. The effort is worth both our time and our best thinking.

NOTES

1. The agreement is the Arrangement on Officially Supported Export Credits, which provides guidelines for export credit practices of the U.S. Export-Import Bank and similar agencies abroad. It is a voluntary arrangement involving 20 OECD member governments and the Commission of the European Community.
2. Organization for Economic Cooperation and Development, *International Investment and Multinational Enterprises,* Paris, 1976.